Attaining Heaven

J. P. McCarthy, S.J.

Attaining Heaven

What It Is *and* How to Get There

SOPHIA INSTITUTE PRESS
Manchester, New Hampshire

Sophia Institute Press
Box 5284, Manchester, NH 03108
1-800-888-9344

www.SophiaInstitute.com

Sophia Institute Press® is a registered trademark of Sophia Institute.

paperback ISBN 978-1-64413-784-0
ebook ISBN 978-1-64413-785-7
Library of Congress Control Number: 2022945318

First printing

Contents

Preface ix

Part One: The Road to Heaven

1. Our Destiny. 5
2. Our Hope. 19
3. The Narrow Gate 37
4. The Reward of Merit 53

Part Two: Heaven

5. The Vision of God 73
6. Bliss. 85
7. The Works of God .101
8. The Resurrection of the Body 117
9. The Incidental Joys of Heaven 131
10. The Achievement .143

Preface

S⎰t. Thomas More, while a prisoner in the Tower, wrote *A Dialogue of Comfort against Tribulation*, in which there occurs the following passage, which will serve as an introduction to this book:

> Cassianus, the very virtuous man, rehearseth in a certain collation of his that a certain holy father in making of a sermon spake of heaven and heavenly things so celestially, that much of his audience with the sweet sound thereof began to forget all the world and fall asleep. Which, when the father beheld, he dissembled their sleeping, and suddenly said unto them, I shall tell you a merry tale. At which word they lift up their heads and hearkened to that, and after the sleep therewith broken heard him tell on of heaven again. In what wise that good father rebuked then their untoward minds so dull unto the thing that all our life we labour for and so quick and lusty toward other trifles, I neither bear in mind nor shall here need to rehearse. But thus much of that matter sufficeth for our purpose, that whereas you demand me whether in tribulation men may not sometime

refresh themself with worldly mirth and recreation, I can no more say but he that cannot long endure to hold up his head and hear talking of heaven except he be now and then between (as though heaven were heaviness) refreshed with a merry foolish tale, there is none other remedy but you must let him have it. Better would I wish it, but I cannot help it. Howbeit, let us by mine advice at the least wise make those kind of recreation as short and as seld as we can. Let them serve us but for sauce and make them not our meat, and let us pray unto God, and all our good friends for us, that we may feel such a savour in the delight of heaven, that in respect of the talking of the joys thereof all worldly recreation be but a grief to think on. And be sure, cousin, that if we might once purchase the grace to come to that point, we never found of worldly recreation so much comfort in a year as we should find in the bethinking us of heaven in less than half an hour.

No one will be inclined to dispute the conclusion of St. Thomas, for he is, in effect, repeating the command of our Lord, "Lay up treasure for yourselves in heaven.... Where your treasure-house is, there your heart is too" (Matt. 6:20–21), or the exhortation of the apostle, "You must lift your thoughts above.... You must be heavenly-minded, not earthly-minded" (Col. 3:1–2). About his story that introduces the conclusion, however, I have more doubt: Was the audience wholly to blame, or did the holy father perhaps make his discourse less interesting than it might have been? Since I am at the moment engaged in laying a book on heaven before the reader, I am acutely conscious of the fact that it is possible to treat of the subject in such a way as rather to induce sleep than to excite an eager attention. I have taken the saint's hint and included a foolish merry tale, but still one merry tale is little sauce for so much meat.

Heaven is a difficult subject. I have more than once decided to preach on heaven and after raking over my thoughts and consulting the books, I have found myself casting about for an easier option. Naturally, the thought came to me that someone should write a book about heaven, but it was long before I made the hesitant step toward trying to write it myself. The reluctance to write about heaven, or to preach about it, comes from one's fear that one must fail to do justice to the subject. Books have, of course, been written about heaven before. There is Dante who brought to the task, with his poetic inspiration, a sound knowledge of theology: I have had to resist the temptation to quote from him at length. Then there is St. Thomas More's *Dialogue,* which I have quoted above. This book is not professedly about heaven, but it does deal with heaven, and I have quoted it several times where I have found that what I was trying to say had been said by St. Thomas with a force and a lightness of touch that my lumbering pen could not hope to match. However, even with this guidance, it is a bold undertaking to write a book about heaven. While pleading, in the time-honored phrase, that there is a long-felt need for such a book, the author dare not claim to meet the need; he must approach his task with the greatest diffidence.

First, then, we must admit that we do not know at all what heaven is like, in the sense that we can form no picture of it. In Holy Scripture we have many vivid images of hell, but of heaven none. Some of the saints, it is true, have had a revelation of heaven and its joys, but they do not tell us what they learnt. Thus St. Paul tells us that he was "carried up into Paradise," and there he learnt "mysteries which man is not allowed to utter" (2 Cor. 12:4). Another who seems to have had a glimpse of heaven was Bl. Roger Wrenno, or Wrennal, a weaver from Chorley, who was executed for his profession of the Catholic Faith at Lancaster in 1616. It is related of him that at his execution, when he had mounted the ladder and the rope had been secured about his neck, the rope broke as he was pushed off and he fell to the ground, stunned for the moment. As he revived, he was offered his life if he would abjure the Faith. For answer, he scrambled to his feet, ran to the ladder, and began to mount, calling for another rope. The executioner, astonished, said to him: "Thou art in a great haste to die." Bl. Roger answered: "If thou hadst seen the things I have just seen, thou wouldst be in as great a haste to die." Well, we have not seen the things that Bl. Roger saw, and nowhere are we given any description of them.

Yet other saints, who have not had the revelations that St. Paul and Bl. Roger had, are scarcely behind them in their eagerness to reach heaven and their appreciation of its joys. Thus it is clear that while we can form no picture of heaven, yet we do know, as I hope to show in the course of this book, a great deal about heaven. What we know of heaven, however, consists almost entirely of spiritual ideas that cannot be grasped without meditation and even then only by one who is not preoccupied with this world and its goods. The preaching of the kingdom of heaven is the whole burden of the teaching of our Lord and His apostles, and it is evident that our Lord intended that the thought of heaven should have for us a firmness, a solidity, and a charm that would support us and lead us on through life.

This book, then, is an attempt to gather together what we know of heaven, of the home that God has prepared for the human spirit. It is essentially a book that gives matter for meditation, and meditation without the most shadowy "Composition of Place." We are told that "no eye has seen, no ear has heard, no human heart conceived the welcome God has prepared for those who love him" (1 Cor. 2:9). Since we shall often have occasion to refer to these words of St. Paul, it may be well to remark here that the apostle and Isaiah, whom he is quoting, are writing not of heaven but of the revelation of the Incarnation. However, the words are traditionally applied to heaven, and it is in this sense that we shall quote them, for they are certainly applicable to heaven. It follows that any human speculation as to what heaven is like must be a waste of time: we must accept what Scripture tells us, meditate upon that, and make no attempt to go beyond it. I have therefore attempted to avoid anything in the nature of speculation that goes beyond the data of revelation, nor have I quoted the guesses of others, even when they are of high authority, although indeed the Doctors of the Church are slow to "guess" and warn us against doing so. In many places there must remain some doubt as to the exact meaning of the revelation we have received, and I hope that I have always indicated clearly my hesitation when I make some statement of which I am less sure. I have at every step sought to fortify myself with quotations from Scripture, even at the risk of being wearisome, though indeed one does not find the texts of Scripture ever losing their freshness: it is the commentator who is more likely to be tiresome. Except in one passage, I have made use of the Knox version throughout, and I should like to say here that this book, such as it is, could scarcely have been written if that version had not been available.

I have divided the book into two parts: part one deals with the road to heaven, part two with heaven itself. Such a division naturally suggests itself and has much to recommend it, although it inevitably involves some repetition, since the same ideas and the same texts must be considered from two different aspects. Also this division is essentially artificial because in the second part, heaven is viewed necessarily from this side of the grave, and part two therefore deals also with the road to heaven. Nonetheless, in this part, the pilgrim is concerned less with the road than with the distant prospect of his goal.

It is, as I said before, with great diffidence that I lay this book before the reader. If he finds it uninspiring, he should realize that the fault lies with the writer and not with the subject, and I venture to suggest that anyone who ignores what I have to say and gives himself to meditation on the texts I adduce will soon deepen his appreciation of heaven. I have cited the main texts, but still only a few of the available texts. Going through the Gospels and the epistles with this in mind, one is amazed by the frequency of reference to heaven and its joys. But I think that it is true also that we ourselves have heaven very often in our thoughts. Whenever we think of death, we cannot but think of heaven; when we pray, we are virtually thinking of heaven; when we make a conscious moral choice, we are equivalently thinking of heaven. We are on the road to heaven. However, the attractions of this world make a direct appeal to eye and ear and heart; those of heaven do not. Heaven is often in our thoughts, but the thoughts touch on it too lightly and pass on. This book is an attempt to give the thought more substance.

Attaining Heaven

PART ONE

THE ROAD TO HEAVEN

ONE

Our Destiny

HEAVEN is the ultimate destiny of man. That is the substance of what we have to say in this chapter, and the statement clarifies at once the nature of man and of his task during his life on earth. First, man, after a few years of this life, has an unending life beyond the grave; he is a traveler, and his destination in which he is to be a permanent resident is of immensely greater importance than his journey thither with its inevitable discomforts and mishaps. But secondly, man is now on the road to heaven, and it is essential for him to take the right road and to travel along it in a fashion that will bring him in due time to his destination. It would be absurd for us to forget our journey's end, but it would be no less ridiculous if we were so preoccupied with the end as to neglect the efforts and precautions necessary to bring our travels to a successful termination. However, the greater danger for us is that we should forget the end and consequently spend ourselves in aimless wandering instead of setting our faces in a definite direction. This chapter, then, is meant to give us our first signpost.

It is natural that Christians, looking at the world from this perspective, should find themselves so often and so much at variance with the good people who are anxious only to "make the world a better place to live in." The Christian does that, but he is not immediately concerned with doing it. When we are asked what Christianity has done in two thousand years, or whether the world is any better now than it was in the time of Christ, we may point to the abolition of slavery, to the emancipation of woman, to free hospitals and schools and refuges, to works of charity whether individual or on a massive scale; we may point to these, or we may reply that Christianity does not set out to make the world a better place to live in. Christians, in making themselves better and better fitted for their heavenly home, necessarily influence their surroundings and their fellow men, but the world as such they do not seek to improve: indeed the world as such they regard as something beyond improving, a snare, an enemy. Our Lord, in the course of His last charge to His apostles, said to them: "If the world hates you, be sure that it hated me before it learned to hate you. If you belonged to the world, the world would know you for its own and love you; it is because you do not belong to the world, because I have singled you out from the midst of the world, that the world hates you" (John 15:18–19), and later He expressly excludes the world from His prayer to the Father: "I am not praying for the world" (John 17:9). The world, then, in a very true sense is hateful to the true follower of Christ. Yet, bad as it is, the world is a very attractive place, and the Christian must ever be seeking to detach himself from it, to be "heavenly-minded" and not "earthly-minded."

We seek to be citizens of heaven, not citizens of this world, and our efforts must be directed toward making us good citizens of heaven. When the modern psychologists tell us to persuade ourselves that we are every day and in every way better and better, or to tell ourselves each morning that this is going to be a wonderful day, and each evening that it has been a wonderful day, we must be slow to lend ourselves to such woolly self-deception. Their "better" is not our "better"; their idea and our idea of a wonderful day are not the same: for them it may be such a thing as influencing others and winning friends; for us it is a matter of laying up treasure in heaven. When scientists, having brought us to the brink of an atomic war, tell us, as some of them do, that our only hope is "to improve human nature," the Christian, who has devoted a lifetime to the uphill task of improving one individual human nature — his own — and who is dissatisfied with the result of his efforts, may be forgiven if he is not sanguine about the success of this proposal. We maintain that the only hope is our hope, the only means of securing real happiness even in this world is our means. Because we reject half-truths, because we have a clear and definite knowledge of what the world is for and what man is for, we have a program for man and for the use man must make of the world.

God made us, and He made us for heaven; He gave us life, formed us, body and soul, for eternity and not for time. An all-wise God designed every part and fitted out the whole that makes up man in such a way that in heaven alone can human nature find its fulfillment and its crown. Since this is so, it is inexpressibly foolish of us to fix our thoughts, aspirations, and efforts on a life that must inevitably end in a few short years, throwing us on the shores of an eternity for which we should now be preparing.

God made us for eternity and yet we cling to life. This is natural to us, part of our nature, and therefore it comes to us from God who made our nature. We are not like other creatures about us — entirely material, corruptible, destined to death. There is in man a soul that is immortal; his power of reasoning, of abstract thought, his free will, his sense of moral obligation, show the existence of an immaterial principle that gives him life. So philosophers have taught and so through the ages men of every race and tribe have believed. Many have seen the future life as a shadowy existence, something less than human; some have looked forward to a very earthly paradise; some, like the Buddhists, have believed in the transmigration of souls, with a series of lives, which find their end at last in a sort of nothingness, where human personality will cease to be; many indeed have hesitated to look for a full immortality, for the spirit of man quails before infinity, which everlasting life implies. It has, however, been reserved for the materialists, who take such an inadequate and one-sided view of man even in this life, to deny to him altogether another life beyond the grave. Apart from such aberrations, mankind as a whole is convinced of the survival of man, the survival of each human personality. This is the conclusion to which reason leads us, and our Faith confirms, clarifies, and amplifies the conclusion, teaching us that God intends man to survive and to be perfected in his true home.

It is then from God that we have this instinct that makes us cling to life, and the instinct is not in vain, for we are immortal. We are mistaken, however, in clinging to this miserable and transitory life on earth, and in not looking forward to that full life that is to come. Not that the fear of death is in itself a thing to be ashamed of, since death is a violent breaking of the union of body and soul, a punishment for sin, a pain to be endured on the road to heaven that God has marked out for us. We may well be afraid of death, but if we take a proper view of it, it will be the sort of fear that we have of the dentist's chair. The saints feared death, but they forgot their fear when they fixed their eyes on the glory that lay beyond it.

God made man for happiness, gave to him free will so that he could choose the means to attain it, but wrote into his heart the moral law to guide him in his quest, for the commandments of God are not fetters placed upon human nature but directives to prevent man from going astray in his journey through life. Man is not sufficient to himself; he must seek his completion, his happiness, outside himself, and too often he grasps at things that can only do him harm. Everywhere and in everything, it is happiness that he seeks, and he looks to find it in riches or in pleasure or in power; everywhere and in everything he is disappointed, for he is striving to satisfy an appetite that is in truth insatiable. Wealth, when attained, brings not happiness but jealousies, anxieties, suspicion, and hate; pleasure brings degradation, cloying of the appetite, frustration as the eagerly sought satisfaction becomes dust in the mouth; power corrupts and brings strife and hatred. Man's very nature seems to drive him forward to disappointment, but in fact it is his haste to grasp at shadows that deceives him. If he would stop to look at himself, to measure the extent of his desires and his capacities, he would know that the good he should seek must be without limit; written in his own heart is the law that should guide him, and it would guide him to God. "Thou hast made us for thyself," St. Augustine says, "and we cannot rest until we rest in Thee." In the knowledge and service of God, man can find such peace of soul as is possible on earth; the possession of God Himself can alone satisfy all man's aspirations, and that is reserved for the life to come.

Man is a social animal; he loves his fellows; he finds his greatest peace in the family, in human friendships, in corporate society. If there is one thing on earth that gives us here below a foretaste of heaven, then it is the happy Christian family, knit together by the closest human ties, united in the service of God and in mutual love, a citadel against the trials of this temporal life. But the trials are always there, and they must eventually disrupt the family itself. Death must come, and even without the intervention of death, there is the slow passing of the years that must at last bring a parting that leaves behind sorrow and vain memories. Sometimes, the parting is postponed too long, and the happy relationship withers in decay. Friendship, too, is a very precious gift from God — giving a mutual support, a solace, a sharing of burdens and of ideas that can bring the greatest happiness — that yet so often brings heavy sorrow. Friendship, too, is necessarily dissolved by time, but quite often it ends prematurely in the bitterness of disillusion, in a miserable estrangement, even in betrayal. The friends may take different paths in life and drift apart; they may take contrary paths and from friends become enemies. The joy of union that man craves, permanent, not subject to partings, not liable to disillusion, is surely promised to him by God, who placed this craving in his nature, but it is promised in the future life and not in this.

Man's nobility is seen above all in his intellect. He dominates the creatures of the world by virtue of his power of searching into the truth of things, mastering every kind of knowledge, attaining wisdom. Perhaps in this age we have lost our respect for those who devote themselves to the higher and more noble branches of knowledge, and we should certainly be going too far if we said that there is always found in man a craving for truth. The infant, indeed, just learning to talk, lisps: "Why? What is it for?" The child, pulling his toys to pieces *to see how they work*, shows the restless activity of the human mind. But the thirst for knowledge seems to have evaporated in the schoolboy who shows a disinclination to learn those things at least that his betters think he should learn, although often enough he shows an undisciplined curiosity in other directions. It is hard to detect devotion to truth in the millions who look for no better intellectual food than their daily newspapers provide for them, or who, if they do look further, are satisfied with the vapid froth of a "digest." One may even doubt whether there is any depth of wisdom in the modern type of "expert" who seeks out and memorizes his catalog of facts, which he might more profitably commit to one of those "thinking machines" that he so ingeniously builds. Yet if it be true—as it undoubtedly is—that the thirst for knowledge is sometimes absent or blunted or perverted, we quickly realize that this means a certain lack of humanity, that the circumstances of this person's upbringing or the warping of his character has been such that he is something less than a man should be. The mind was made for knowledge, but it may be deflected from the pursuit or the attainment of knowledge by man's own inertia, or by an environment of misery or destitution or brutality or indeed of luxury. Man can debase his mind by sophistry or falsehood or allow it to become atrophied by neglect. But if we look back at the history of the human race, we find that the great names that stand out are those of the philosophers and teachers, of the poets and statesmen, of the artists and men of science, who have acquired a mastery over some field of knowledge, who have held firmly to the path of truth and have in consequence been able to exert a beneficent influence on their fellow men. However this may be, this faculty is part of man's nature, and its capacity seems almost without limit. Yet in this life it goes unused or half used, or badly used. Even the wisest is liable to be deceived and to fall into error. This God-given power that distinguishes man from beast can only rest in truth; in this life, it will not find rest.

To sum up what we have said so far, when we look at man, the highest of God's creatures here on earth, we must pronounce him a misfit and a monstrosity, if we leave heaven out of account. Man possesses powers and aptitudes that cannot be fully exercised in this world as we know it. The life of each individual man must be misdirected unless it is aimed at heaven. We are sometimes lost in wonder at the design and order in the universe; at the eye, for instance, built up from a little cell, growing and developing to its amazing complexity, yet so marvelously adapted to its ultimate purpose; at the flower, often so beautiful and so fragrant, fertilized by such intricate agencies, producing the little seed that can again give rise to a new plant. We wonder at these marvels of creation and are led by them to praise the all-wise Creator. Is it to be thought of that in His highest and noblest work, His hand should have failed Him, that man, made in the image of his Maker should not have awaiting him beyond the grave the home for which his spirit craves? God made man and He made him for heaven.

I

God made all things for His own great glory. Before He created, there was nothing except God; even after creation there is nothing worthy of comparison with Him; He could have had no other purpose but His own glory when He freely created. All His creatures, fulfilling their natures, sing His praises. Man alone is *free* to glorify his Creator: not of necessity, yet bound by law, must he praise God. God made all things for His own great glory, but He has so bound up the good of man with His own glory that man, freely glorifying God, attains the perfection of his being. Fulfilling the law of God, knowing Him, praising Him, loving Him, man is fulfilling the law of his own destiny, and the all-wise Creator has attached sanctions to His law so that neglect of it will bring retribution, but submission to it will bring reward.

Now it follows from this that when we argue, as we have done, that man's reward is not to be received in this life, that the crown and perfection of his being will be attained only in heaven, we are not saying anything to belittle the importance of this life; on the contrary, we are expressing and emphasizing its very real importance. Man is not here on earth to amuse himself, to find some tawdry satisfaction in things that are so much beneath him; his life and his actions have an eternal value hereafter. God made us for heaven, but He has placed us on earth; He bids us lay up to ourselves treasure in heaven, but the treasure must be won and accumulated here and now. Heaven is our goal, and we must keep it before our eyes, lest we be so attracted by the things of earth as to give ourselves up to the pursuit of them for their own sakes. The earth is our place of trial, and we shall win heaven by doing our duty now.

It follows, then, that the enemies of God, who call religion "the opium of the people," are slandering religion. Their meaning is that religion so sets men's minds on the future life as to make them neglect this life with its duties and responsibilities. Those who make the accusation are materialists who would place the be-all and end-all of human life in this material world, who think that concern for a future life turns men's minds away from themselves and their plans. It is no part of our purpose to refute material-ism, but we must insist that this accusation against true religion is without the slightest foundation in fact. It is true certainly that the thought of heaven will make a man turn in disgust from the terrestrial paradise that is promised by the materialist, but, on the other hand, the heaven to which he looks forward makes him fully a citizen of this world and the best of citizens. To attain heaven, he must serve God, obey His commandments, follow the teaching of our Divine Lord. How different would be the world today if these ideals were acknowledged and followed!

In our lifetime, we have seen the usurpation of absolute power, deification of the state, suppression of elementary human rights: all this would have been impossible to men who acknowledged the rights of God Himself, Lord and Creator of all. We have seen mass murder, unspeakable cruelty, slavery reborn in a form that would have shocked even the ancient pagans; this could not be if men saw in their fellow men heirs of heaven. Marriage is debased, homes broken up, the basis of the stability of society is destroyed, by those who do not know that men are heirs of heaven. We have to complain of juvenile delinquency because the little ones of Christ have been scandalized. Greed has bred strife between nations. That godlike gift of man, speech, the power of communicating his thoughts to his fellows, has been discredited by systematic lying, until a man's word becomes a weapon of deception and peace is made impossible. Riches are piled up while the poor starve and live in misery. Vice is exploited without thought of the corruption that must follow.

Now these evils have not been perpetrated by those who have their eyes fixed on heaven. On the contrary, they know that they must give to every man his due, that they must reject pride, selfishness, greed, falsehood, injustice, luxury. "You know well enough," St. Paul warns us, "that wrongdoers will not inherit God's kingdom. Make no mistake about it; it is not the debauched, the idolaters, the adulterous, it is not the effeminate, the sinners against nature, the dishonest, the misers, the drunkards, the bitter of speech, the extortioners that will inherit the kingdom of God" (1 Cor. 6:9-10). That was and remains Christian teaching, and if it were put in practice, how different the world would be! Then the rulers and all who are called to take some part in governing the state would remember that they are not supreme, above all law, but that they receive their authority from God; that they must govern in accordance with His laws; that they remain answerable to Him for their actions; that those subject to them exist not for the good of the state but to attain the destiny for which God made them; that the state must help its subjects in every way it can and never hinder them in the pursuit of this destiny. The manufacturer or businessman; the professional man, doctor, lawyer, or teacher; the employee, craftsman, workman, each of these should be obedient to the law of God, aiming at the end of human life, looking to the judgment to come. Each of them must earn his living, each provide for his own family, but all owe debts to one another, debts dictated by justice and charity. They must not be at strife with one another but united, not seeking to circumvent one another but lending mutual support to one another, each looking no doubt to his own rights but all ready to acknowledge the rights of others. Again, parents, whose marriage has been blessed and sanctified by God, will be united in love, conscious of the high office that God has conferred on them, bringing up their children in the knowledge of their duties to God and to their fellow men and with the character training that will carry them through the difficulties and temptations that they must meet in life.

This might be the description of the model citizen; it is actually the Christian teaching of the way to live in order to attain heaven. Is it not then nonsense to talk of religion as "the opium of the people"?

II

In saying all this, we do not of course deny that in practice many Christians fall far short of what they should be, that all at times fall short so that the ideal is not attained. This does not, however, weaken the argument set out above, for it shows that we need more religion and not less in our daily lives; but it does bear very sharply on the purpose of this book. We know that our true home is in heaven, but we easily forget it or are half-hearted in our efforts to reach our goal. We tell ourselves, with some conviction, that this is a miserable world, yet we find it or some of the things in it extraordinarily attractive, and we allow ourselves to be led astray by them from the path that would lead to salvation. It is easy for us to persuade ourselves that we can make the best of both worlds, as the saying is, but we are deceiving ourselves if we do, for very often we must find that the good things of life cannot be purchased without guilt; we must sacrifice them if we would attain to heaven. St. Thomas More, in a characteristic passage, rebukes those chaplains to great men, who allow their patrons to gratify their passions in this life, while yet promising them salvation in the next:

> And in such wise deal they with him as the mother doth sometime with her child, which, when the little boy will not rise in time for her but lie still abed and slug, and when he is up weepeth because he hath lien so long, fearing to be beaten at school for his late coming thither, she telleth him then that it is but early days, and he shall come time enough, and biddeth him: Go, good son, I warrant thee, I have sent to thy master myself; take thy bread and butter with thee, thou shalt not be beaten at all. And thus, so she may send him merry forth at the door that he weep not in her sight at home, she studieth not much upon the matter though he be taken tardy and beaten when he cometh to school. Surely thus, I fear me, fare there many friars and state's chaplains too, in comfort giving to great men when they be loath to displease them. I cannot commend their thus doing, but surely I fear me thus they do. (*Dialogue*, I, 14)

No doubt it is easier for the chaplain to a great man to humor him, rather than to attempt to check him in his evil courses, and it is easier, too, for each of us to stifle conscience, to indulge our appetites, to trust that all will come right in the end. It is easier, but it is a terrible mistake. Our Lord holds out no hope to us that we can make the best of both worlds. In the parable of Dives, the rich man who feasted sumptuously every day, and Lazarus who lay at his gate, covered with sores, wishing that he could feed on the crumbs that fell from the rich man's table, the latter died and was carried by angels to Abraham's bosom while Dives died, too, and found his grave in hell. And Abraham said to Dives: "My son, remember that thou didst receive thy good fortune in thy life-time, and Lazarus, no less, his ill fortune; now he is in comfort, thou in torment" (Luke 16:19ff.). Our Lord condemns the Pharisees who do their works of piety, pray, fast, to be seen by men and honored by them: they have their reward and can look for none from their Father in heaven. He would have us be in the world and yet not belong to the world.

This raises for us a very real difficulty and one that will remain with us as long as we live. Our destiny is to be attained in the life to come, yet we have a very real work to do here and now and it seems to absorb all our attention. What is it, then, that God wants of us? God wants a man here on earth to live his own individual life, certainly, growing to maturity, studying, fitting himself to earn his living, working; he wants of most men that they should marry and exercise all the duties of the head of a family; he expects a man to take a full part in social life — too many Christians neglect that duty — perhaps political life, fulfilling the duties of charity in cooperation with his fellows. All this God asks of a man, but He requires that all should be done in accordance with His laws, that is, in brief, in accordance with the Ten Commandments. It is to this full human life, lived in the sight of God and amounting in truth to a life of service of God that the reward of heaven is promised. It is no use pretending that this will be easy. We shall return to the difficulty later, but for the present it is enough to say that obedience to the commandments will necessarily set a man against the way of the world, will bring him into opposition to those to whom this world is everything. If he has his eyes on his ultimate destiny, he will despise the world and what it has to offer.

Yet, in such a life, a man can find real satisfaction and peace. It remains true that sadness and disappointment, sacrifice and fruitless effort, pain and sorrow are man's portion on earth, but the climber on the mountainside makes his effort gladly, and the sight of the goal lightens the difficulties of the road. Even in his work here, a man finds happiness, not unalloyed but still very real. He was placed here by God, given a work to do that he is doing to the best of his ability; he finds himself imperfect but perfectible, leaning to evil but capable of holiness. Giving himself to the services marked out for him by his Maker, he is conscious of accomplishment, of peace of soul, of progress toward his goal.

TWO

Our Hope

I N the last chapter, we examined the nature of man as we know it in ourselves, and we drew the conclusion that man's life is destined to find its crown in a future life. We did not go on to attempt to deduce what that future life would be like, and it would have been useless for us to do so, for although it would be possible from a comprehensive view of man to deduce his natural destiny, we know by God's revelation that the heaven He has prepared for us is far beyond the requirements of human nature, beyond our dreams. Human nature, as such, would be fittingly rewarded by some sort of natural paradise, but human nature was from the beginning raised to a supernatural state and thereby given a right to a supernatural paradise. God gave this supernatural life to Adam for himself and for all his descendants. Adam, indeed, by his sin, lost it for himself and for us, but through the grace of Christ, it is restored to us, and with it, a new heaven is opened to us. It is of this that we say: "No eye has seen, no ear has heard, no human heart conceived, the welcome God has prepared for those who love him (1 Cor. 2:9), for by our natural powers, we simply cannot conceive what this supernatural life or this heaven is.

This supernatural life is given to us now. We live, even here on earth, a life no mere man could live. What is this life? The answer to that question we can find only in God's revelation. Holy Scripture then tells us that it is the very life of Christ: "I am alive; or rather, not I; it is Christ that lives in me. True, I am living here and now, this mortal life; but my real life is the faith I have in the Son of God, who loved me, and gave himself for me (Gal. 2:20). We belong to Christ, we have put on the person of Christ, we are God's sons (Gal. 3:27). We are shrines of the Holy Ghost (1 Cor. 6:19), temples of God (2 Cor. 6:16). We are made sharers of the divine nature (2 Pet. 1:4). These are a few of the texts that tell us of the transformation that is effected in man by the grace of Christ. A necessary consequence of this change in man is that the heaven to which we look forward is not one that befits a man, but the inheritance of Christ Himself: "You are no longer exiles, then, or aliens; the saints are your fellow citizens, you belong to God's household" (Eph. 2:19). We are "heirs of God, sharing the inheritance of Christ" (Rom. 8:17). All these passages refer to the change produced in our souls by grace in this life, here on earth. We might put it this way: an angel, looking down from heaven upon us, sees indeed the stains of the world but, looking at our souls enriched with the grace of Christ, sees in them the divine likeness that marks us as children of God, sees the family resemblance to the only-begotten Son of God, recognizes us as fellow citizens.

Now any form of life is recognized by the corresponding activity. If, for instance, we take a little shriveled seed and plant it and water it, and if it swells up and sprouts and grows, we see at once that it was not, as it appeared to be, a morsel of inert matter, but a seed with true vegetable life. If, again, we look at what seems to be a piece of wood or perhaps a leaf, and if we touch it and see it move itself away, then we know at once that we were deceived, that the thing we were looking at was one of those insects that resembles a twig or a leaf; for only an animal has this power of sensitive reaction and self-movement. So, from a man we expect those signs of reason and intelligence that distinguish a man from an animal.

Thus, then, having received supernatural grace and the very life of Christ, we must show a Christlike activity. He is, He tells us Himself, the vine and we are the branches, drawing, as it were, their lifeblood and their fruitfulness from Him: "I am the vine, you are its branches; if a man lives on in me, and I in him, then he will yield abundant fruit; separated from me, you have no power to do anything. If a man does not live on in me, he can only be like a branch that is cast off and withers away; such a branch is picked up and thrown into the fire, to burn there" (John 15:5–6).

St. Paul develops the same teaching under a metaphor that makes us the organs of a body of which Christ is the head: "United to that head of ours, on which all the body depends, supplied and unified by joint and ligament, and so growing up with a growth that is divine" (Col. 2:19), and again: "We are to follow the truth in a spirit of charity, and so grow up, in everything, into a due proportion with Christ, who is our head. On him all the body depends; it is organized and unified by each contact with the source which supplies it; and thus, each limb receiving the active power it needs, it achieves its natural growth, building itself up through charity" (Eph. 4:15–16).

We are then the members, the limbs of Christ, living with His life, growing through our union with Him. Our thoughts are His thoughts: "Not that, left to ourselves, we are able to frame any thought as coming from ourselves; all our ability comes from God" (2 Cor. 3:5). Our will is His will: "Both the will to do it and the accomplishment of that will are something which God accomplishes in you, to carry out his loving purpose" (Phil. 2:13).

Without Him, we cannot think, we cannot will, we have "no power to do anything." We continue to live a human life, which to human eyes is unchanged, but without Christ the supernatural life cannot continue. Because it is, in the strictest sense, supernatural, it follows that it is invisible to human eyes and beyond the recognition of natural consciousness and experience. It cannot be described in human words: it is for this reason that our Lord and His apostles make use of metaphors to explain it to us.

With this new mode of life and new activity, we must have a new way of knowing, and this we have through divine faith, which is defined by the *Catechism* as "a supernatural gift of God, which enables us to believe without doubting whatever God has revealed." Faith is a virtue, poured into our souls at Baptism, a virtue not acquired by laborious effort as are the natural virtues but coming to us by the free gift of God, the first of the graces of Christ. It can grow like other virtues in the soul, but again, unlike natural virtues, it can grow not through purely human effort but by fresh grace from God. It is only, for instance, by faith that we know or could know all that is set out above about the supernatural life. When we have explained it as fully as we can, it remains obscure to our human minds, and yet it is grasped by faith as certain truth. We believe it because God has revealed it.

I

It was necessary to set out thus briefly the nature of the supernatural life as an introduction to this chapter in which we treat of our hope of heaven, since the heaven we hope for corresponds to this new life in our souls. With faith, then, God gives us the gift of hope, which is defined as "a supernatural gift of God, by which we firmly trust that God will give us eternal life and all the means necessary to obtain it, if we do what He requires of us."

In our ordinary natural life, we are accustomed to the sentiment of hope that attaches itself to an absent good, to something desired but not possessed, which is attainable but with difficulty. Hope is necessary to man. His life depends upon it, for life is activity and he is moved to activity by his hopes; every effort whether of mind or of body is made in order to attain to something for which he hopes. There is always something more that he wants, or if, for the moment, he has all that he desires, yet he hopes that his present wellbeing will continue. But more often there is something wanted to make life worthwhile, and if he ceases to hope, then the very will to live is sapped. The dreamer may indulge in vain, fantastic hopes; when he is disappointed in them, he keeps himself going with a new dream. The practical man has learnt to measure out his hopes according to the means that lie in his power, and attuning his efforts to his hopes, he works to attain them and thus reaches some degree of contentment. The magnanimous set their hopes high and often attain to greatness. The heroic and outstanding achievements of man in every field of activity are due to hope, which raised him to superhuman effort because he thought achievement possible, because he hoped. There was, to take one example, that poor Chinese sailor who during the war drifted alone on a raft in the Atlantic, keeping himself alive for several months by catching fish with a bent pin, sucking their juices for drink and eating their flesh for food. Because he continued to hope for survival, he displayed a remarkable ingenuity, incredible endurance, and steadfast courage. He lived, where a lesser man would have despaired and died.

Hope elevates the mind, gives firmness to the will and determination in the face of difficulties. It is for these reasons, after all, that this book is written, to direct our minds to our eternal hope, that we may be unmoved by the trials we have to undergo, unattracted by the distractions of the world, set firmly on the road we must follow in order to reach our goal.

When Adam sinned, all hope was lost, and heaven was closed to man. God at once hastened to give new hope with the promise of a Redeemer who should open heaven to us once more. Supernatural hope is a grace that can only come to us from God, through Christ. Further, it is directed to God in that we look to His power and mercy to bring us to the life in heaven that is beyond man's powers, beyond even his aspirations. Finally, it is centered in God Himself, for the possession of God is the heaven we hope for: "Eternal life is knowing thee, who art the only true God, and Jesus Christ whom thou hast sent" (John 17:3). We hope to attain to heaven, across the obstacles and difficulties of this life, in spite of our weakness, in spite of sin, through the help of God. We hope again that, through God's grace, we shall overcome the temptations that lead to sin, for we know that sin is the one obstacle that could wreck our efforts. We can hope, too, for temporal favors that God may give to His children to smooth their path on the way to heaven.

Hope then is the guide and principle of all our efforts toward the salvation of our souls. By hope, our eyes are set upon our only good, God Himself, and contemplating Him, we grow in His love and are detached from transitory goods that we may seek our true beatitude. Looking at our goal, we see how powerless we are to reach it, so much beyond human strength is it, but at the same time we realize the power and goodness of God, which beckons us on and assures us of divine strength. We see, too, that God will not save us without our cooperation, and through hope, we are brought to make the necessary effort so as to make our salvation secure.

Since the virtues of faith and hope are so essential to us in the way of salvation, the providence of God has made a certain disposition in regard to them. If a man falls into mortal sin, the soul dies—that is, loses supernatural life, sanctifying grace, and the other permanent gifts of God; but it retains faith and hope. By this condescension of God to our weakness, the sinner continues to believe in Him and to hope in Him. Hence it is possible for the soul in sin to turn again to God known by faith, to be raised up by hope, and so to come by God's help to penance and to the recovery of a full supernatural life.

Our Lord throughout His public life awakens hope in the hearts of His hearers. From the Sermon on the Mount, the promise of heaven is an essential part of His preaching: "Be glad and light-hearted, for a rich reward awaits you in heaven" (Matt. 5:12). The burden of His teaching is: The kingdom of heaven is at hand, and this is the message that He sends His apostles to give to the people. Our Lord, however, was met by a misunderstanding that remained throughout His life. The Jews and even the apostles themselves had a very earthly hope of the restoration of the kingdom of Israel. He was the King of Israel, but they were very slow to grasp the fact that His kingdom was not of this world. He made it clear from the beginning that the kingdom was one that the poor and the meek would inherit (Matt. 5). Later, after they had seen His miracles and power, He told the apostles that His kingdom must be established by His Passion and death, but this they would not understand (Matt. 16). On the night of the Last Supper, when He was just about to open heaven for us by His death, He expressed clearly to them the promise that is our hope: "Do not let your heart be distressed; as you have faith in God, have faith in me. There are many dwelling-places in my Father's house; otherwise, should I have said to you, I am going to prepare a home for you? And though I do go away to prepare you a home, I am coming back; and then I will take you to myself, so that you may be where I am" (John 14:1–4), and: "After a little while you will see me no longer, and again after a little while you will have sight of me. Believe me when I tell you this, you will weep and lament while the world rejoices; you will be distressed, but your distress shall be turned into joy.... One day I will see you again, and then your hearts will be glad; and your gladness will be one which nobody can take away from you" (John 16:19–22). In these words of our Blessed Lord, there is in truth a very full revelation of the nature of heaven, and we shall return to them later to examine them more fully, but for the present they are cited as the promise that is the foundation of our hope. The apostles, overwhelmed by the events of the Passion, were unable to hope. Even later, after the Resurrection, they returned to their old hope for the kingdom of Israel, and they asked about it even on the day of the Ascension (Acts 1:6), but when the Holy Spirit came upon them, He taught them all truth and banished their foolish hopes of an earthly kingdom, once and for all.

The apostles had been told to "preach the gospel," and consequently we find constantly that our Lord's words are repeated, expanded, and explained in their teaching of the early Christians. Thus St. Paul eloquently celebrates the virtue of hope and the sure promise of salvation, especially in his Letter to the Romans. We will quote at length from this magnificent passage:

> Once justified, then, on the ground of our faith, let us enjoy peace with God through our Lord Jesus Christ, as it was through him that we have obtained access, by faith, to that grace in which we stand. We are confident in the hope of attaining glory as the sons of God; nay, we are confident even over our afflictions, knowing well that affliction gives rise to endurance, and endurance gives proof of our faith, and a proved faith gives ground for hope. Nor does this hope delude us; the love of God has been poured out in our hearts by the Holy Spirit, whom we have received. (Rom. 5:1–5)

We rejoice in our certain hope, he says; we rejoice even in affliction, which is overcome by hope; the Holy Spirit Himself guarantees our hope. The apostle then goes on to prove the certainty of our hope from our redemption by Christ: "Were that hope vain, why did Christ, in his own appointed time, undergo death for us sinners, while we were still powerless to help ourselves?... All the more surely, then, now that we have found justification through his blood, shall we be saved, through him, from God's displeasure. Enemies of God, we were reconciled to him through his Son's death; reconciled to him, we are surer than ever of finding salvation in his Son's life" (Rom. 5:6, 9–10). There was hope even when we were sinners, for Christ died to redeem us from sin; now that we are no longer sinners, we are doubly sure of our salvation. He goes on to explain the economy of the Redemption and argues from the Fall of Adam and of all his descendants with him, setting against this the New Adam, Christ our Lord, by whom we are brought again to life: "One man commits a fault, and it brings condemnation upon all; one man makes amends, and it brings to all justification, that is, life" (Rom. 5:18). After a digression in the next two chapters, which we need not follow, St. Paul returns in the eighth chapter to his praise of hope:

Those who follow the leading of God's Spirit are all God's sons; the spirit you have now received is not, as of old, a spirit of slavery, to govern you by fear; it is the spirit of adoption which makes us cry out, Abba, Father. The Spirit himself assures our spirit, that we are children of God; and if we are his children, then we are his heirs too; heirs of God, sharing the inheritance of Christ; only we must share his sufferings, if we are to share his glory. Not that I count these present sufferings as the measure of that glory which is to be revealed in us.... Hope would not be hope at all if its object were in view; how could a man still hope for something which he sees? And if we are hoping for something still unseen, then we need endurance to wait for it.... Meanwhile we are well assured that everything helps to secure the good of those who love God.... All those who from the first were known to him, he has destined from the first to be moulded into the image of his Son, who is thus to become the eldest born among many brethren.... Who can be our adversary, if God is on our side? He did not even spare his own Son, but gave him up for us all; and must not that gift be accompanied by the gift of all else?... Who will pass sentence against us, when Jesus Christ, who died, nay, has risen again, and sits at the right hand of God, is pleading for us?" (Rom. 8:14-34)

Such then is the glory of our hope. In the words of our Lord at the Last Supper, on the night before He died for us, He seems to appeal to us to put our faith in His love, and, here, St. Paul seems to echo that appeal: God did not spare His own Son, and giving Him has He not given us all else? St. Paul then closes this magnificent passage with a defiant proclamation of the certainty of our hope:

Who will separate us from the love of Christ? Will affliction, or distress, or persecution, or hunger, or nakedness, or peril, or the sword?... Of this I am fully persuaded; neither death nor life, no angels or principalities or powers, neither what is present nor what is to come, no force whatever; neither the height above us nor the depth beneath us, nor any other created thing, will be able to separate us from the love of God, which comes to us in Christ Jesus our Lord. (Rom. 8:35-39)

II

Our hope for heaven is certain, and therefore our hope in God for all the means necessary to attain heaven is certain also. All the graces that we need are ours for the asking, even without the asking; yet it is right that we should ask. We owe praise and thanksgiving to God, but we owe it to Him, too, to bring our petitions to His feet; doing so, we are acknowledging that all good comes from Him. "Believe me," our Lord said, "you have only to make any request of the Father in my name, and he will grant it to you" (John 16:23). Yet it is often our experience that we ask and do not receive. Why? It must surely be that we ask for the wrong things; often our petitions are too lightly made. For grace, for faith, for hope, for charity, for anything that helps to our salvation, we may pray boldly and with the certainty that we shall be heard. But if we pray for other things, for temporal favors, for instance, or even for spiritual comfort and consolation, He may grant our prayer or He may not, for He is all-wise and we are not, and He may see that what we ask would be bad for us, would hinder our eternal salvation. Then, indeed, He will not grant our prayer but will give us instead a grace that meets our needs, for the one thing necessary to us is eternal salvation, and other things pale in insignificance in comparison with that.

It is true, of course, that in this life we have many needs and we are right in bringing them to our loving Father, but we do so knowing how little able we are to grasp their relative importance and to separate the trivial from the essential. The little child, for instance, has endless petitions to make; the boy and girl at school, poring over their books, or neglecting them, pray for success at games, or for fine weather, or for holidays. We smile at their immaturity, but I do not know that we are right, for even a small child may be acquiring habits that will be a support or else a plague in all the life that follows, and every action flowing from a human will, however immature, is recorded and will be weighed by the Judge in the eternal scales. But all ask God for favors, great or small: the lovers pray for removal of obstacles to their marriage, for a house; the mother prays for her sick child; the student prays for success in an examination on which his career depends; the father of a family prays for the means that will enable him to fulfill his obligations; we all pray for comfort, or for delivery from trouble and danger. What is there for which prayer is not made? And all these prayers are, or can well be, true worship of God, for they show the children going in confidence to a loving Father.

Our Lord told us to be as little children and, in these prayers, we are. Yet He knows and we know too, although we sometimes forget, the one thing necessary, and therefore these prayers must always be conditional, whether we express the condition or no: we pray that God may give us what we ask if it is His will and for our good. Anything that does not help, that hinders, our salvation is then a thing not asked. So many people pray, for instance, for success in examinations and do not succeed that we may well suspect that many souls are helped to salvation by failure in examinations. So many pray for the recovery of some dear one from sickness that, if the prayer were not conditional, we should seem to be flouting divine wisdom, which alone knows the fitting time to call each soul to judgment and reward. There is perhaps no kind of prayer so often made and left unheard as that for worldly advancement, for some position, for money or financial advantage of some kind. On this we must recall our Lord's solemn warning: "With what difficulty will those who have riches enter God's kingdom! It is easier for a camel to pass through a needle's eye than for a man to enter the kingdom of God when he is rich" (Luke 18:24-25). A man has reason rather to be afraid if he finds riches coming to him and accumulating, although it is true that man has need of this world's goods, that all must seek a competency. The Church when she finds people in destitution hastens to relieve their temporal necessities, for a starving man finds little leisure to think of his soul. The father of a family, who is hard-pressed and in continual anxiety about money, is not free to fulfill his more important duties to his family. It is certainly not wrong then to pray for relief to God, but He may know that poverty and anxiety are good for us. So, too, when we pray to be delivered from trouble or sickness or pain of one kind or another, God may see that it is better for us to carry our cross. He never loses sight of our real good; we ourselves so easily do. In all our prayers, therefore, we must leave the issue entirely in His hands. Looking back upon our lives, we can see how complicated their pattern has been, and we can often perceive the graces by which God has guided us on a path we did not foresee. So the future, and especially our salvation, can be made secure only by God's graces: some of those graces will be known to us and we can ask for them, but others will be unknown, and in what we ask we shall certainly make mistakes. Our hope is not in our own strength, nor in our own wisdom, but in the strength and wisdom of God: He will assuredly give us all the graces that we shall need.

III

Our hope for heaven, then, and for the means by which we can attain it, is firm and certain. The graces we need we shall receive, but given the grace of God, our own cooperation is necessary. Can we trust ourselves? Nothing, as St. Paul assures us, can separate us from the love of God, but we can separate ourselves by mortal sin. St. Paul himself was afraid that "I, who have preached to others, may myself be rejected as worthless" (1 Cor. 9:27), and he exhorts us to work out our salvation "in anxious fear" (Phil. 2:12). This fear of ourselves is not to be lightly put aside; indeed, it must not be put aside at all, for here is the crisis of our life on earth. God, who made us, has a right to our service, lays on us commandments that we ought to obey, but leaves us free to disobey His commandments, to refuse our service. For our service and obedience, He offers us the reward of heaven; if we disobey, we incur the penalty of damnation. The choice is ours. Our inattention to the task before us, our preoccupation with the petty cares and pleasures of this world, our insensibility to our own fate, will not alter the urgency of that choice. We go on our way through life, but at the end heaven or hell awaits us, certainly, inevitably. We do well to fear.

So long as we dwell on earth, the thought of hell can never be far distant when we think of heaven. We fear for ourselves, we fear the weakness of our own wills, we fear God's justice, but it is a salutary fear. The revelation of hell is itself a grace given us by the mercy of God. Hell, painted by our Lord in vivid words, holds us back from sin and plants our feet on the way to heaven. We should not, then, fly from the thought but, on the contrary, cherish it, dwell upon it, draw from it the strength to resist temptation. We shall continue the more securely on the way to heaven if we realize that the way to hell is open to us and that it is the easier road. We do well to fear.

The urgency of our choice is impressed upon us by our Lord in all His teaching. Was it not this that brought Him into the world, when we were helpless to help ourselves? Was it not this that brought Him to His death, that He might save us from eternal death? He warns us against those things that may beguile us, lead us astray: "Do not lay up to yourselves treasures on earth" (Matt. 6:19). "How is a man the better for it, if he gain the whole world at the cost of losing his own soul?" (Matt. 16:26). Those who would make their salvation secure must despise and even fly from riches;

they must always be on the watch for the wiles of the devil; they must hate the world and be hated by it. We must watch and pray that we enter not into temptation.

But on the other hand, if our path through life is beset with dangers and pitfalls, our Divine Lord has provided the helps and remedies to enable us to avoid and overcome them. This He has done especially by the sacraments, which He gives to us as the instruments of our salvation. In Baptism, original sin and all past actual sins are blotted out, we become children of God, and we acquire a right to all graces necessary for salvation. The sacrament of Penance is the God-given remedy for our weakness and makes it possible for us, if we fall into fresh mortal sin, to wash it away in the sacrament and recover our supernatural life. Confirmation strengthens us to fight the good fight, to be soldiers of Christ, waging the endless war of Christ with the world. The sacrament of Matrimony, while instituted to bring into the world new citizens for heaven, is also a remedy for concupiscence. The Holy Eucharist, above all, is food for our souls and sanctifies our bodies; it is the sacrament of our resurrection, the pledge of eternal life; our Lord tells us: "The man who eats my flesh and drinks my blood enjoys eternal life, and I will raise him up at the last day" (John 6:55). Holy Orders gives to men a priesthood to offer up to God the great sacrifice of our redemption and to bring the gifts of God to us, for our Lord, mediator of God and men, left His representatives on earth that He might, through them, continue visibly His work of sanctifying us and leading us to heaven. Finally, in Extreme Unction, we are strengthened to meet death and prepared immediately for heaven by the cleansing away of the last vestiges of sin. Our Lord knew all our needs, all our weaknesses, and He made provision for them all. If we neglect His sacraments, then we have reason to fear, but if we use them, we are secure.

Again, in the communion of saints, we have the support of those who have gone before us, and we have a special assurance in our Lord's giving us His own Mother to be our Mother. He earned for us the graces by which we are to be saved; He has placed them in her hands to distribute them to us as we need them. More wise than any earthly mother, more concerned for our welfare, more powerful to assist us, she waits for us to turn to her for help, knowing that the duty and office of motherhood were laid on her by her divine Son. Pray for us sinners now; at every instant of our lives we need her care, and we receive it. Pray for us at the hour of our death; then most of all we need her prayers, for on that moment, and on the state of our souls at our passing, depends our eternity. We cannot foresee the end; we cannot have any notion of how or when it will come; we can but leave it in her hands. But leaving it in her hands, we can have no grounds for craven fear.

There is certainly a price to be paid for our salvation, and that we shall consider more fully in the next chapter, but the knowledge of our own weakness should not dim the brightness of our hope. It should take away pride, reliance on our own efforts; it should fill us with humility, yet also with confidence in the grace of Christ; it should move us to make, with His help, the efforts that will bring us salvation. "Bestir yourselves then, brethren, ever more eagerly," says St. Peter, "to ratify God's calling and choice of you by a life well lived; if you do this, you will make no false step, and it will be no grudging entrance that is afforded to you into the kingdom of our Lord and Saviour Jesus Christ" (2 Pet. 1:10–11). And St. Paul echoes much the same thought: "He who thinks he stands firmly should beware of a fall. I pray that no temptation may come upon you that is beyond man's strength. Not that God will play you false; he will not allow you to be tempted beyond your powers. With the temptation itself, he will ordain the issue of it, and enable you to hold your own" (1 Cor. 10:12–13). God allows us to be tempted, but He allows it for our good: He is at hand to help us and to give us strength to overcome any trial; He will not play us false.

We must conclude, therefore, that although it is possible for us to turn from God by mortal sin and to fling away our hope of heaven, we can only do so by base ingratitude to our Divine Lord, by ignoring the graces He has heaped upon us and daily heaps upon us, by neglecting the sacraments, by refusing the love of His Mother and ours. We can go forward then with every confidence yet working out our salvation with anxious fear, not presumptuous but trusting in God, pressing on along the road to heaven. If God is with us, who can be against us?

THREE

The Narrow Gate

CHRIST, our Lord, died for the salvation of all mankind, and we know from Scripture that it is God's will that all men should be saved (1 Tim. 2:4). Yet a man's salvation can only be secured by his own cooperation with grace, for God has given to him free will, and his service of God must be that of a free agent. It remains in the power of man to reject the graces of God and to go willfully on the road to perdition.

Our life on earth, then, is no picnic; we have a serious work to do, and our Divine Lord does not hide from us the fact that it is a difficult and arduous work. In His Sermon on the Mount, He gives the warning: "Make your way in by the narrow gate. It is a broad gate and a wide road that leads on to perdition, and those who go in that way are many indeed; but how small is the gate, how narrow the road that leads on to life, and how few there are that find it" (Matt. 7:13–14). Our Lord does not say in this text that there are few who are saved; what He asserts is that there are few who walk in the secure but difficult way that leads to salvation. There may be many who are far from the way of salvation in this life, who yet find grace in the end: we do not know the bounds of God's mercy. On one occasion this question, which many of us would like to ask, was put to Him directly—"Lord, is it only a few that are to be saved?"—and He declined to answer it, merely repeating the words: "Fight your way in at the narrow door; I tell you, there are many who will try and will not be able to enter" (Luke 13:23-24). It appears from this and other texts that God does not wish to reveal to us the number of the saved.

We do not know the bounds of God's mercy, but this we do know for certain, that He will judge most severely those who have received the greater graces. No one, and especially no one who has received great graces, has any ground for complacency. We have the gravest warning in our Lord's denunciation of the scribes and Pharisees:

> The scribes and Pharisees, he said, have established themselves in the place from which Moses used to teach; do what they tell you, then, continue to observe what they tell you, but do not imitate their actions, for they tell you one thing and do another.... Woe upon you, scribes and Pharisees, you hypocrites that shut the door of the kingdom of heaven in men's faces; you will neither enter yourselves, nor let others enter when they would.... Serpents that you are, brood of vipers, how should you escape the award of hell? (Matt. 23)

Our Lord's meekness and His gentleness with sinners are often emphasized, and rightly, so long as we do not forget that He could also speak in terrible wrath. These men were hypocrites, looking for the praise of men and careless of God's judgments, expounding the law to others while neglecting it themselves except in outward show. "Brood of vipers, how should you escape the award of hell?" It will go hard, He says, at the Day of Judgment with Capernaum,

Bethsaida, Corozain, those cities that have heard His preaching and seen His miracles, far harder for them than for the pagan cities of Tyre and Sidon, or even for Sodom itself, the city of wickedness. The apostles themselves were the salt of the earth, but He warns them that, if the salt lose its taste, it is good for nothing but to be thrown out and trampled underfoot. When He had given them the parable of the faithful servant who watched for his lord's coming, Peter asked Him if the parable was for the apostles or for all men, and He answered: "It is the servant who knew his Lord's will, and did not make ready for him, or do his will, that will have many strokes of the lash; he who did not know of it, yet earned a beating, will have only a few. Much will be asked of the man to whom much has been given; more will be expected of him because he was entrusted with more" (Luke 12:47–48). A man who was scandalized and perverted even in childhood, who was brought up in the midst of crime and vice, is not beyond the limits of God's mercy. We cannot know what graces may go out to him at the last, as grace went out to the penitent thief, who, by the revelation of God, was able to see the divinity of this Man, who was dying like himself as a criminal on the Cross. On the other hand, one who has known our Lord, known His Church, received His sacraments, had all the helps He has left us to bring us to heaven, to one who has had all these, and has neglected or rejected them, will there be still more graces to come? God is very merciful, but He is just. We must strive to enter at the narrow gate.

I

When our Lord was sending out His apostles to preach, He said, in the course of His charge to them: "He is not worthy of me, that does not take up his cross and follow me" and then He added some words, which He was to repeat to them so often that we cannot doubt that they were meant to convey an important lesson, a lesson on this subject that we are discussing. He said: "He who secures his own life will lose it; it is the man who loses his life for my sake that will secure it" (Matt. 10:39). Some time later, after Peter's confession at Caesarea Philippi, He used almost the same words: "If any man has a mind to come my way, let him renounce self, and take up his cross, and follow me," adding again, "The man who tries to save his life shall lose it; it is the man who loses his life for my sake that will secure it" (Matt. 16:24-25). Our Lord's words on this occasion are recorded by St. Mark also (Mark 8:35) and St. Luke (Luke 9:24). St. Luke reports the words yet again, apparently in the course of our Lord's final journey up to Jerusalem (Luke 17:33). St. John does not mention any of these addresses by our Lord, but he tells us that He used the same words in Jerusalem, after His triumphant entry on Palm Sunday: "He who loves his life will lose it; he who is an enemy of his own life in this world will keep it, so as to live eternally" (John 12:25). These words, then, were often on our Lord's lips when He was teaching His apostles, and they must have a central place in His gospel. In the six texts in which we find them recorded in the Gospels, there is nowhere any attempt to soften them, but rather they are emphasized and driven home. As to their meaning, the text in St. John removes any possible ambiguity: a man must be the enemy of his own natural life in this world if he would secure his supernatural, eternal life; the man who loves his natural life in this world will lose his life eternally.

The words are verified exactly and literally in the martyrs, who die for the sake of our Lord and thus gain eternal life, and it has often happened that a martyr has been given the choice between death and renouncing the Faith, between mortal sin and martyrdom, between death for the body or death for the soul. God may ask a soul to pay this price for salvation, as our Lord did when the sons of Zebedee asked Him for the chief places in His kingdom, and He answered: "Have you strength to drink of the cup I am to drink of, to be baptized with the baptism I am to be baptized with?" (Mark 10:38). Martyrdom is a privilege given only to a few, although in the state the world is in today there is no one who can be quite sure that the call may not come to him, but there is no doubt that those who receive the call are abundantly prepared and strengthened by God's grace. The words of our Lord that we are considering, however, have a wider application: to every Christian there is presented the choice between giving himself to the enjoyment of the present life and despising the present life that he may gain eternal life. St. Paul puts this teaching of our Lord before all his converts: "If you live a life of nature, you are marked out for death; if you mortify the ways of nature through the power of the Spirit, you will have life" (Rom. 8:13). What he means by the life of nature is clear from many passages in his epistles; for instance, he writes again:

> We too, all of us, were once of their company; our life was bounded by natural appetites, and we did what corrupt nature or our own calculation would have us do, with God's displeasure for our birthright, like other men. How rich God is in mercy, with what an excess of love he loved us! Our sins had made dead men of us, and he, in giving life to Christ, gave life to us too; it is his grace that has saved you; raised us up too, enthroned us too above the heavens, in Christ Jesus. (Eph. 2:3-6)

Nature is corrupt; to follow the ways of nature is to sin. St. Paul then constantly exhorts his Christians to cherish the new life they have found in Christ, to be dead to the world, dead to sin, dead to self-love, that they may live to Christ.

A person brought up from infancy as a Catholic, accustomed to regard the demands of religion and right living as the very framework of his life, may not always be fully conscious of what he is renouncing, but it remains true that a real Christian is bound by restraints and held back by laws that make it impossible for him to give himself, as the children of this world give themselves, to an unhampered enjoyment of life on earth. Those who come to the Faith later in life are much more alive to the discipline and the constraints to which they must submit. The Christian must, as we have seen, make his living as others do; he will, in general, marry and bring up a family; he must provide for them and for himself; he must therefore seek for advancement in his career or profession whatever it may be. Yet his devotion to his career must always remain a secondary thing with him; the means he uses for his advancement are governed and restricted by God's laws; he must renounce pleasures and eschew practices that others think legitimate; he sees duties to his family that others do not know; he must be in the world but not of it. There is an immense difference between making a career the prime object of all one's efforts and regarding it as a secondary thing, subordinate, even incidental, to the main business of life. Our modern psychologists have taught us to talk about our scales of values, but, for the Christian, there must be only one real value, in comparison with which all the rest are negligible.

The Church is truly Catholic in every sense, and Catholics are therefore to be found in every walk of life and in every profession in which they can legitimately engage. Yet it has been said that in certain professions and lines of achievement, Catholics are not as numerous nor as prominent as their numbers suggest that they should be—as captains of industry, for example, or as leading scientists. It may be so. Whatever his worldly profession, a good

Catholic can never give himself to it with complete abandon or single-minded devotion. He has something more important to think about, and it may very well be that this is an obstacle to outstanding success in such an absorbing career as scientific research. We have argued elsewhere that the Christian is the best of citizens, and we would maintain that that remains true, for though the world might overlook other shortcomings in a man if he accomplished more in some direction such as scientific discovery, we cannot admit that the world's view is right. Scientific research at its best is a seeking for truth, and as such we applaud it, but we believe that there are higher truths, much more important for a man to know. We tend to be children of our age, and all of us are too prone to take the world's views as sound, but we should know from our own experience and also from our Lord's words that the world is commonly wrong. The world concentrates on the present and thinks that alone important; we look to the future life to which the present is only a stepping-stone. We must be ready to lose the present that we may gain the future.

We said in the first chapter that the service that God asks of us is summed up in the observance of the commandments. That is true: if we keep the commandments, we are on the road to heaven, but we shall not keep the commandments unless we are dead to the world. The living death to which our Lord called His followers is no exaggeration. The Church, knowing us, imposes on us the duty of mortification, abstinence on Fridays, fasting in Lent, and so on. If, in modern times, the law of fasting has been relaxed and at times suspended, this is not because the Church thinks that we do not need mortification, but because it appears that the circumstances of the time impose upon us sufficient hardship or because the variety of the conditions of modern life make it difficult to frame a general law, binding upon all. Without mortification, the

Christian life cannot be lived. Given the weakness of our nature and the false glitter of the world, the commandments must be a continuous rein upon our desires and passions. We must be constantly pulling our wills back to the path marked out by the law of God; we must be saying no to ourselves when nature would pull us the wrong way and perhaps as often saying yes when nature would prefer inertia; we must be refusing what life offers and choosing what nature shrinks from. Only so can we live in Christ.

With the hardships involved in the observance of the commandments, the ordinary misfortunes of life, too, impose a constant curb on nature, if we would but recognize it and embrace it. It is true of course that the misfortunes and sufferings of life come to all, good and bad alike, for God "makes his sun rise on the evil and equally on the good, his rain fall on the just and equally on the unjust" (Matt. 5:45), but the spirit in which they are received is different, and it is this that makes of them either calamities or crosses. The children of the world, while they seize on the good things of life for their own selfish advantage, try to avoid or to minimize the afflictions; if they cannot do that, they will grumble at them or curse them. It is the humble spirit that accepts the misfortune, and kisses the hand of God that sends it, that transforms the affliction into a saving cross. For true mortification lies in the continual submission of our wills to God's will, in the determination to trample on self-will whenever and wherever it is found to be at variance with the will of God. To the worldling this will seem to be a living death, but in it is to be found true life. The soul on the way to heaven must carry a cross.

We have but to keep the commandments, but the first of these is: "Thou shalt love the Lord thy God, with thy whole heart and thy whole soul and thy whole mind," and our Lord leaves us in no doubt that God is to be preferred to everything, that it will be necessary at times to choose between God and what is dearest to us, and that, when it is necessary, it will cost us much:

> If thy hand or thy foot is an occasion of falling to thee, cut it off and cast it away from thee; better for thee to enter into life crippled or lame, than to have two hands or two feet when thou art cast into eternal fire. And if thy eye is an occasion of falling to thee, pluck it out and cast it away from thee; better for thee to enter into life with one eye, than to have two eyes when thou art cast into the fires of hell. (Matt. 18:8–9)

This means surely that there is no sacrifice that we must not be prepared to make in order to secure our salvation and to avoid offending God by mortal sin. The sacrifices that He does demand of us are not often as dramatic as this, but as we have seen, He does ask of some souls the sacrifice of their lives; even now, in many parts of the world, He is asking His faithful followers to suffer persecution, loss of property, imprisonment, and death for His name's sake. God sends His trials in proportion to our strength, and with the trial He gives, too, the grace to overcome it: He will not allow us to be tempted beyond our powers. However, we cannot promise ourselves ease and comfort, nor must we look for peace on earth:

> Do not imagine that I have come to bring peace to the earth; I have come to bring a sword, not peace. I have come to set a man at variance with his father, and the daughter with her mother, and the daughter-in-law with her mother-in-law; a man's enemies shall be the people of his own house. He is not worthy of me, that loves father or mother more; he is not worthy of me that loves son or daughter more; he is not worthy of me, that does not take

up his cross and follow me. He who secures his own life
will lose it; it is the man who loses his life for my sake that
will secure it. (Matt. 10:34–39)

The coming of our Lord brought peace on earth to men of goodwill, but not peace between men of goodwill and bad. The road
to heaven, although it can never be an easy road, is often pursued
in happy union with those who are dear to us, but often again it
does demand renunciation of those we love, for always we must so
love God as to be ready to sacrifice everything for His sake, if He
should demand it. Heaven is the pearl of great price for which a
man must be prepared to sell all that he has that he may purchase it.

II

The harshness of this call of our Divine Lord to carry the cross is
softened and sweetened by His example and by the motive of love
that vivifies the Christian life. Thus He drew on the sons of Zebedee
with His question: "Have you strength to drink of the cup I am to
drink of?" and to all of us He says: "He that has a mind to follow me,
let him take up his cross," and it is this that His apostles put before
us: "If you do wrong," says St. Peter, "and are punished for it, your
patience is nothing to boast of; it is the patience of the innocent
sufferer that wins credit in God's sight. Indeed you are engaged to
this by the call of Christ; he suffered for our sakes, and left you his
own example; you were to follow in his footsteps" (1 Pet. 2:20), and
St. Paul tells us we are "heirs of God, sharing the inheritance of
Christ; only we must share his sufferings, if we are to share his glory"
(Rom. 8:17). In the Cross of Christ we have the greatest proof of
His love for us, and those who love Him desire to be united with
Him in suffering. This is the aspect of the cross that appealed to the
saints, and this explains why they had such an appetite for suffering,

mortifying the flesh in food, in sleep, in avoidance of every comfort; explains why they distrusted prosperity in this world; and explains why they despised the passing things of time. We will quote again, as an example, St. Thomas More:

> Now to this great glory can there no man come headless. Our head is Christ; and therefore to Him must we be joined, and as members of His must we follow Him if we will come thither. He is our guide to guide us thither and is entered in before us, and he, therefore, that will enter in after, *debet sicut ille ambulavit et ipse ambulare,* the same way that Christ walked, the same way must he walk. And what was the way by which He walked into heaven? Himself sheweth what way it was that His Father had provided for Him, where He said unto the two disciples going toward the castle of Emmaus: *Nome haec oportuit pati Christum et ita intrare in gloriam suam?* Knew you not that Christ must suffer passion and by that way enter into His kingdom? Who can for very shame desire to enter into the kingdom of Christ with ease when Himself entered not into His own without pain? (*Dialogue,* III, 26)

It seems almost as if in pain and suffering there was something of positive good. Certainly, we cannot doubt that it is good for human nature in its present state, the state bequeathed to us by the sin of Adam. It was by sin that suffering came to man, and by suffering sin is expiated. Nothing defiled can enter heaven, and therefore suffering is necessary to the sinner. But apart from the necessity of expiation, it seems that ease and comfort and pleasure act as snares for man, lead him to find satisfaction in this life, and, worse than that, lead him to pride. When we enjoy good health, when all our undertakings prosper, when life is smooth and pleasant and easy, we take all the credit to ourselves, congratulate ourselves that we have planned so well; we listen willingly to the plaudits of others; we become proud, and the proud man is taking to himself the glory that belongs to God. He is satisfied with the present life and is not prepared to make the least sacrifice for the world to come. He is lost. In sickness and pain, on the other hand, we know our weakness; in frustration and disappointment, we realize how powerless we are; in humiliation, we find humility. We know ourselves for sinners, for creatures of God, for children who look to their Father for help. Without the cross, should we find our way to heaven? Should we not be content with the earth and what it offers? We know that our Lord chose for Himself and for us the way of the cross; we may well doubt whether He could have safely given to us any other road. Those who ask why there is so much misery and pain in the world, why God created so imperfect a world, consider this world as an end in itself, but this world is not an end in itself. If the world is looked on as an arena where heaven must be earned, if it is taken together with the heaven that is its completion, then surely it must be admitted that it is not a bad world at all. He is a rash man who tries to conceive of a better; he knows little of human nature who thinks it could safely be made more comfortable.

III

The road to heaven, then, is a hard road, but it is very far from being a dreary road. For, first of all, it is a road and not a place of repose: one does not expect the comforts of home on the highway. Then it is the road to heaven, and the glory that awaits us at the end is a support to us in any rigors we have to endure, whatever they may be. When one thinks of the labor and scheming and hardship that men will undergo in order to amass riches that they can enjoy for a few short years at most, or of the long years of study, privation, and self-denial that they will devote to securing advancement in some profession, or of the vexations and indignities they will put up with in order to win some coveted office, when one thinks of these and compares them with our trials on the one hand and our prize on the other, one cannot doubt that we are making the easier choice, as well as the wiser.

It was with this promise of the future, as we have already seen, that our Lord consoled His apostles:

> Believe me when I tell you this, you will weep and lament while the world rejoices; you will be distressed, but your distress shall be turned into joy. A woman in childbirth feels distress, because now her time has come; but when she has borne her child, she does not remember the distress any longer, so glad is she that a man has been born into the world. So it is with you, you are distressed now; but one day I will see you again, and then your hearts will be glad; and your gladness will be one which nobody can take away from you. (John 16:20–22)

In the years that followed, the apostles had abundant experience of the trials and persecutions that our Lord had promised them, but they, too, consoled their converts with the same promise: "We are to share an inheritance," writes St. Peter,

> that is incorruptible, inviolable, unfading. It is stored up for you in heaven, and meanwhile, through your faith, the power of God affords you safe conduct till you reach it, this salvation which is waiting to be disclosed at the end of time. Then you will be triumphant. What if you have trials of many sorts to sadden your hearts in this brief interval? That must needs happen, so that you may give proof of

your faith, a much more precious thing than the gold we
test by fire; proof which will bring you praise, and glory,
and honour when Jesus Christ is revealed. (1 Pet. 1:4–7).

And St. Paul, who suffered so much, says, "This light and momentary affliction brings with it a reward multiplied every way, loading
us with everlasting glory" (2 Cor. 4:17).

We have then the satisfaction of knowing that we are progress-
ing toward our goal, and that a goal for which no sacrifice can be
too great. But besides this, our Lord promises us consolation even
in this life: "Come to me, all you that labour and are burdened; I
will give you rest. Take my yoke upon yourselves, and learn from
me; I am gentle and humble of heart; and you shall find rest for
your souls. For my yoke is easy, and my burden is light" (Matt.
11:28–30). His followers are always experiencing the truth of this
promise. They may fear the constraint of the yoke before they take
it upon themselves, but when they have accepted it, they find that
it is easy. They shrink from the burden, but shouldering it, they
discover that it is light. Truly, however, His most precious gift is the
peace of soul that follows the learning of His lesson of gentleness
and humility of heart. "Peace," He says, "is my bequest to you, and
the peace which I give you is mine to give; I do not give peace as
the world gives it" (John 14:27). The peace that the world gives is
an uneasy peace, found in grasping anxiously what often eludes
the grasp, in holding desperately what can never satisfy the heart
of man, in forgetting death, in shutting the eyes to judgment, in
stifling conscience. On the other hand, those who submit to the
yoke of Christ find a new peace, new vistas open up before them,
everything in life falling into place; life itself is given unity and
purpose; pain is made fruitful; trials are made rich; death itself,
though not shorn of its fear, can yet be made welcome as a step

to heaven. The Christian can say to himself, "I am doing what a man should be doing; I am where God wants me to be; I suffer what God wants me to suffer; I do what God wants me to do; in everything I suffer, in everything I do, God's grace is working in me, enabling me to suffer and to do." Not at war with the world but bowing before the hand of God, not wrestling with adversity but submitting to it, not setting himself up on a pedestal from which he must fall but remaining close to earth, gentle and humble of heart, he finds rest for his soul. Even if some great affliction comes upon him, the death for instance of some dear relative, which to the worldling would be unrelieved calamity, he finds, with the deepest sorrow, peace.

A sacrifice made for Christ may be painful, but it always brings peace: further than that, it very often brings, mysteriously, joy. We know that on the Cross Christ our Lord, in the extremity of His agony of soul and body, did not cease to enjoy in His human soul the Beatific Vision, which is the joy of the blessed. It seems to be His will that His members, too, should know this union of sorrow and happiness, pain and joy, and we meet it constantly in the lives of the saints. For example, St. Bonaventure, in describing the incident when St. Francis of Assisi received the stigmata, tells us that sorrow pierced his heart like a sword, while, at the same time, his whole soul was filled with joy. In our own small way, we sometimes experience something of this sort and learn that the peace of Christ can fill us with true happiness. God did not mean us to find our heaven in this world, but He did mean us to be happy here, to receive a foretaste of heaven, to live at peace with ourselves and with Him, as His children should. The Christian life calls for death to this world, but we die so that, even here on earth, we may have life and have it more abundantly.

FOUR

The Reward of Merit

THERE is an old story of a man who died and went up to heaven. He knocked at the gate and was admitted, though somewhat grudgingly, by St. Peter, who asked one of the angels, attendant at the gate for this purpose, to show the new arrival to his mansion. The angel led him through the streets of heaven with their dazzling mansions built of precious stones; the very streets were paved with precious stones, so that he could scarcely believe that heaven itself could be so beautiful. As they went on, they came to streets where all the mansions were built of purest gold; these gave way to mansions of silver, then to handsome villas of cut stone, and finally, to the newcomer's surprise, to plain bricks and mortar and even to ferroconcrete. But still they went on until at last, on the very outskirts of the celestial city, the angel pointed out to him his mansion, a mere shack built of a few boards nailed together, with, believe it or not, a corrugated iron roof. When he was assigned to this accommodation, the poor soul could not altogether hide his disappointment, and the angel, noticing it, said to him: "Yes, I am afraid it is a poor sort of place, but, you know, we did the very best we could with the materials you sent up."

In this story, there is this much of truth that our mansion in heaven is built of our own materials; if we would have treasure in heaven, we must lay it up now. We merit heaven by our life on earth. Merit, as we use the word here, may be defined as a right to a supernatural reward, arising from a good work done freely for God under the influence of grace because of the promise of God that guarantees this reward. We are speaking then of merit in the full sense, of something that is owed in return for our works and not merely given out of liberality; of a supernatural reward that is an increase of sanctifying grace and finally heaven itself; and we make the claim to a reward for our merits in virtue of God's promise. We find in fact that in Holy Scripture heaven is constantly described as the reward of our good works, the remuneration for our service, the wages for the day's labor, the prize for our efforts, the crown to be won.

"To thee, Lord, mercy belongs; thou wilt repay every man the reward of his deeds" (Ps. 61:13). We find mention of heaven as a reward in our Lord's words from the very beginning of His teaching with the eight Beatitudes in the Sermon on the Mount: "Blessed are you, when men revile you and persecute you, and speak all manner of evil against you falsely, because of me. Be glad and light-hearted, for a rich reward awaits you in heaven" (Matt. 5:11-12). He tells the multitude that they must not do their good works of prayer, of fasting, of almsgiving, before men who will honor them for it, but secretly so that "thy Father who sees what is done in secret, will reward thee" (Matt. 6:18). They are to lay up to themselves treasure in heaven, for "where your treasure-house is, there your heart is too" (Matt. 6:21). They are to make it their first care to seek the kingdom of heaven: so doing they will save their souls. "How is a man the better for it, if he gains the whole world at the cost of losing his own soul? For a man's soul, what price can be high enough? The Son of Man will come hereafter in his Father's glory with his angels about him, and he will recompense everyone, then, according to his works" (Matt. 16:26–27). Even to give a cup of cold water in His name will bring reward (Matt. 10:42), while "every man that has forsaken home, or brothers, or sisters, or father, or mother, or wife, or children, or lands for my name's sake, shall receive his reward a hundredfold, and obtain everlasting life" (Matt. 19:29). He makes it quite clear that this reward is, in the strict sense, recompense: "Why, lift up your eyes, I tell you, and look at the fields, they are white with the promise of harvest already. The wages paid to him who reaps this harvest, the crop he gathers in, is eternal life, in which sower and reaper are to rejoice together" (John 4:35–36). Here, it is true, our Lord is speaking especially to the apostles, but in His description of the judgment He says that the reward is given to all the just because they fed the hungry, clothed the naked, and so forth.

St. Paul often repeats this promise of our Lord. In the fifteenth chapter of the First Letter to the Corinthians, in which he treats of the resurrection of the body, a chapter we shall have occasion to quote later on, his final words are: "stand firm, then, my beloved brethren, immovable in your resolve, doing your full share continually in the task the Lord has given you, since you know that your labour in the Lord's service cannot be spent in vain" (1 Cor. 15:58). Here heaven is promised precisely as a reward for the service we render to the Lord by our life in this world. Again, in the Letter to the Hebrews, there is a passage that recalls our Lord's words on the judgment and the reward of those who feed the hungry: "God is not an unjust God, that He should forget all you have done, all the charity you have shewn in his name, you who have ministered, and still minister, to the needs of his saints" (Heb. 6:10). In this passage, the reward is claimed as due in justice from God; it is due in justice because God has promised it: "Do not throw away that confidence of yours, with its rich hope of reward; you still need endurance, if you are to attain the prize God has promised to those who do his will" (Heb. 10:35–36). So in many other passages in St. Paul, some of which we quote elsewhere, there is a promise of reward for good works done in the service of God, a reward that we can claim in justice, since God has promised it, a reward that we must earn in this life, for after death comes the judgment.

We seem to have been laboring this point, but it was necessary to do so, for many objections have been raised against this doctrine that heaven is given to us in reward for our good works. It is argued that this makes our motive mercenary and unworthy of the service of God; that the service of God is something that, as His creatures, we owe Him; that we can give God no service that is in any way of use to Him or of which He has need; that this doctrine makes us selfish; that there should be an equivalence between a service and its reward, whereas all our actions are so utterly worthless in the sight of God that they cannot possibly merit heaven. We will consider each of these objections in turn, and that will serve to make clearer this doctrine of the merit of good works.

First, however, we must say that we should not dare to speak of our merit, of our good works earning the glory of heaven, unless our Divine Lord Himself had taught us to do so. It is not that we are entering an unsupported claim; we are, as we said above, appealing to His own promise of reward for our good works, a promise by which He has bound Himself so straitly that St. Paul can appeal to His justice in support of his own claim to the crown. Where a title rests upon a promise, freely given, it is true that the promise need not have been given; yet after it has been given, the person rendering the service has a right in justice to the reward that was promised. If, for example, an article is lost and a reward is offered for its recovery, then the person who returns it has a strict right to the reward. It is in this way that God has bound Himself to reward us.

I

Is this claim to a reward mercenary and unworthy? It is enough to say that our Lord did not think it so, but the objection really arises from our modern conditions in which the employee is often a wage slave, who does his work because he must and receives the pay for which he has bargained. Even in human relationships we can see that this is wrong. In a more gracious age there was the old retainer, who received a wage indeed but who was regarded as one of the family, whose services were given and received in a spirit of affection; again there was the family lawyer or doctor, who received his fees, for he must live, but whose relations with his client or patient were those of a friend. Now our relations with God are those of children with their Father, to whom we owe everything, and it is our love for Him, and not any spirit of bargaining, that moves us to serve Him.

It is true that all that we are, all that we have, belongs to Him. It is true again that we can give Him nothing that He needs, nothing that is useful to Him, that to speak of our service is something of a metaphor, for we are unprofitable servants. What God asks of us is glory; He has made us free, and in freely observing His commandments, we glorify Him. It is a little thing, but it is what His law demands of us. Now it is the part of a wise legislator to attach sanctions to his laws, punishments for those who break them, rewards for those who observe them. God, therefore, most wise of legislators, is but faithful to His own justice in instituting the reward of good works.

Even this statement that we have just made is open to misunderstanding, unless we recall that His first commandment is

"Thou shalt love the Lord thy God," and that the reward that He promises us is eternal union with Him in love, for this is what heaven means. Loving us, God has given us the grace to love Him in return, and He seeks to make this love eternal. We serve God because we love Him; loving Him, we cannot but seek to be united with Him eternally. What God wants from us is love: what we seek from Him is love. We are then very far removed from the mercenary wage slave bargaining for his price.

The objection that this doctrine makes us selfish, when examined, is seen to rest on a quite false notion of the nature of selfishness. In seeking to attain to heaven, we are seeking to possess the greatest possible Good, and we are therefore showing love of self. But selfishness is not simply love of self; it is inordinate love of self; not simply a desire for our own good but a putting of ourselves before others, even before God. In general, we recognize selfishness easily enough: a child who snatches at something he should share with another, the trader who pursues a line of business that will bring him money though it may bring misery to others, the man who will not give to others in need from his own superfluity—all these are selfish, and the world itself condemns such selfishness. It is in our attitude to our neighbors that selfishness is most clearly shown. They are men like us, creatures of God, with the same needs, the same aspirations, the same destiny; it is vain for us to pretend to love God if we do not love these creatures of God. It is in this form that St. John puts so forcibly our Lord's command to us to love our neighbor: "If a man boasts of loving God, while he hates his brother, he is a liar. He has seen his brother, and has no love for him; what love can he have for the God he has never seen?" (1 John 4:20). But selfishness exists, too, even when there is no question of injury to one's neighbor, in a person who seeks pleasure and satisfaction, in one for instance who eats greedily, in one who is eager to be thought well of, who desires applause, in one who avidly seeks money or power. Such people, of course, must eventually injure others, for the habit of selfishness, acquired by repeated actions, looks always to its own advantage and is indifferent to the advantage of others; yet even when this element of injury to another is missing, the selfishness is still there. The evil seems to be that the person is making his own immediate good the end of his action: he is putting himself where God and God alone should be. The man who refuses to tell a lie in order to save another, the man who would prefer to see his family suffer poverty rather than better them by dishonesty, we do not call these selfish. They are not selfish, because their actions are well-ordered, directed to the end to which they should be directed, that is, God.

Such then is selfishness: a hateful thing that deprives God and our neighbor of what we want to keep for ourselves; a short-sighted thing, too, which looks to immediate gains and is blind to the future. Now, it cannot be said that our desire of heaven falls under this condemnation of selfishness. It deprives our neighbor of nothing; it gives God His due. It involves indeed a love of self, but it is a love of self that we are bound to have, which is imposed on us by our very humanity. After all, our Lord's command to us is that we should love our neighbor as ourselves, implying that we should love ourselves, and we necessarily do love ourselves with a love that reaches to the very depth of our being. If you consider, for instance, your own feelings when you say, "I wish I were you," or "I wish I were in his place," at a time when you see someone else enjoying exceptional good fortune, you will see that what you want is a like good fortune, but happening to you. You cannot conceive, nor desire, a complete change of yourself into someone else, and you can get no satisfaction or even rational meaning from the thought. We are ourselves and we desire good things for ourselves — that is, we love ourselves.

Even in the natural order, we are bound to love ourselves. Among all normal men, suicide is condemned as an unnatural self-hatred. We must take reasonable care of our health, exert ourselves vigorously to preserve life, even work and plan to attain and to keep a certain status of material prosperity. In the supernatural order, we are bound to desire and to work to procure our eternal salvation. We have seen that the whole plan of God's creation of man and the human nature He has given to him require that man should serve God and, glorifying God by his service, should earn for himself salvation. God made us what we are, and the love of self involved in this striving to fulfill our destiny is a well-ordered self-love, a necessary part of our being.

The last objection — namely, that there is no equivalence between our good works and the reward we look for — is fundamental to the whole economy of our redemption. There is a sense in which our actions may be called worthless, yet to say that they cannot be compared to the reward of heaven is to belittle the work that God has accomplished in us through our Lord, Jesus Christ. Through the Redemption, we are sharers in the life of the Son of God, and as the sufferings of our Lord were of infinite worth, so our service and our sufferings take their value from the fact that they are the service of the children of God, of the brethren of Jesus Christ. We say that the sufferings of our Lord were of infinite worth; now, it would not be true to say that the sufferings were themselves infinite, for our Lord suffered in His created human body and soul, and a created nature is not capable of infinity. But the infinite dignity of the Person who suffered, the incarnate Son of God, raises the expiatory and meritorious value of His sufferings so that we rightly call it infinite. The fruit of the work that Christ accomplished for us is given to us in Baptism when we are incorporated in Him and begin to live with His life. Having His grace in our souls, we are brethren of Christ, our actions are His actions, we are already His coheirs, we have a strict right to citizenship in heaven. Our good works really merit heaven, and therefore God's goodness and mercy is not shown in giving us heaven in reward for our good works but, before this, in His giving us supernatural life or, before this again, when He gave us His only-begotten Son. "He did not even spare his own Son, but gave him up for us all; and must not that gift be accompanied by the gift of all else?" (Rom. 8:32). The wonderful transformation that Christ effects in us takes place not when we enter heaven but when we first receive supernatural life. It is not therefore so much that our service here is given the recompense of heaven as that death is not an interruption of our life in Christ. Our supernatural life is begun here and veiled; in heaven it is revealed and crowned.

This, too, explains why we must suffer and why sufferings merit bliss. Christ suffered in expiation of the sins of men, for sin deserves death; in His obedience to death, He made satisfaction for our sins and at the same time, by His submission to the Father's will, merited the grace that gives us life. The disciple is not above his Master; having His life within us, we follow Him in expiation and in merit, and we can dare to say with St. Paul: "I am glad of my sufferings on your behalf, as, in this mortal frame of mine, I help to pay off the debt which the afflictions of Christ still leave to be paid, for the sake of his body, the Church" (Col. 1:24). Christ suffered and died once, but His appetite for suffering is unassuaged; it is His will to continue His work of redemption to the end of time. He continues, then, to suffer but in His members.

What we have been saying does take us far beyond the thought of reward, and it is true that His faithful followers do not look for recompense. They think only of His love for them and, moved to love in return, strive only to follow Him and to be united with Him. It is He who insists that the reward shall be given to those who take up their cross and follow Him. Certainly it is quite false to say that we are magnifying our own good works, for He is the vine, we the branches; without Him we have no power to do anything; yet with Him we can do all things. Our good works are the works of Christ; we live now not we, but Christ lives in us. The reward we hope for is a share in His glory.

II

What are the conditions that must be fulfilled if our good works are to merit heaven? First, merit is only possible while we are in this life: "The night is coming, when there is no working any more" (John 9:4). When we die, there follows at once the judgment, and by our actions in this life, our eternal fate is settled. In the graphic phrase of Ecclesiastes: "North or south as the tree falls, north or south the trunk will lie" (Eccles. 11:3). This is God's will, and in this life He has provided for us abundant opportunities for merit when the complete man, body and soul, is working out his destiny.

Secondly, in order to merit, we must be in a state of grace. This is clear, from what has been said above, that our ability to merit at all depends upon our being living members of Christ, branches not cut off from the vine. Sin, mortal sin, necessarily blots out all previous merit, for no one can be at the same time a child of hell and heir to heaven. Most theologians, however, teach that when a sinner repents of his sin, he receives back all his previous merits. They base this teaching on certain texts of Scripture, for example, "Sinner that will leave his sinning, no harm shall he have" (Ezek. 33:12), and a text from the Letter to the Hebrews that we have already quoted: "God is not an unjust God, that he should forget all you have done." In the context of this passage, it seems that the apostle is exhorting sinners to repentance and promising them that their past good works will be remembered by God.

Finally, it is evident that the work that merits must be a good work and supernatural: only what is good can have the vivifying help of grace. No doubt, in our free acts, our wills are often remiss and our motives mixed, but we hope that a merciful Father may find in such actions something to reward, though by wholehearted service and fervent wills we might greatly increase our merits. Also it can be said that every action that is not sinful is an action of a child of God, and so we may look for merit even from the most ordinary duties of our daily lives. Thus Christ, our Lord, merited when He was a babe at Bethlehem, when He was a child at Nazareth subject to His parents, merited by every action of His life, though we attribute the abundance of His merits especially to His death, for in His death He offered Himself in sacrifice for the sins of mankind.

Because He was constituted head of the human race, our Divine Lord could merit for others; this we cannot do, for merit is a personal thing, and the reward goes to the person who merits it. We can pray for others, but any merit earned when we pray is our own and cannot be given to others. We can make satisfaction for the sins of others, as we do when we gain indulgences for the souls in purgatory, but again the merit of the good work is our own.

Such then is the doctrine of merit, a doctrine full of consolation. Rightly understood, it cannot make us selfish, for we do not make our own happiness our end; although we know that God will reward us, we seek only to serve Him, and we find our happiness in this life and in the next in doing His will. Such an attitude is possible to us only if we love Him, and those who really love Him do not measure out their good works but are ready to give all that He may ask.

III

We may consider here the question that arises from the difference of merit that must exist between souls and the consequent differences in the rewards they receive in heaven. As to the fact, there can be no doubt. Our Lord tells the apostles: "There are many dwelling places in my Father's house" (John 14:2), and St. Paul writes: "And this is my prayer for you; may your love grow richer and richer yet" (Phil. 1:9), while St. John, in the book of Revelation, hears the voice saying: "I am coming soon; and with me comes the award I make, repaying each man according to the life he has lived" (Rev. 22:12). We differ then in love, in grace, in merit; each will be repaid according to the life he led; there are different awards awaiting us in heaven. The question is, does not this conflict with the happiness of heaven? Can there be perfect happiness when there is inequality between the blessed, a giving to one of something that is withheld from another?

It must be answered, in the first place, that this inequality is the will of God, and as we pray, "Thy will be done on earth as it is in heaven," we cannot for a moment imagine that the blessed can fall short of perfect union with the will of God. Their happiness consists of union with that will; the very differences that they see between themselves, since they are God's will, give them joy. Nor can we imagine that in the abode of the blessed there can be any envy or jealousy; nor yet that there can be any repining because they have not made better use of their opportunities when they were on earth. Joy will be unalloyed.

The truth is that each soul entering heaven receives the glory of which it is capable, and its capacity is determined by the fullness of the supernatural life to which it has attained. Now, our supernatural life begins with the first free gift of grace that we receive, normally through the sacrament of Baptism. Some souls die immediately after this and enter heaven without having had any further chance of meriting fresh degrees of grace. On the other hand, some may live a long life and may devote it completely to the service of God, continuously meriting fresh graces, receiving the sacraments, giving themselves wholeheartedly to all manner of good works, performing acts of fervent love of God, perhaps crowning their lives by martyrdom. We can guess at the differences there must be between the pure soul of a newly baptized infant and the soul of a St. Paul, a St. Bernard, St. Francis Xavier, St. Teresa, and we know that the supernatural life of grace is a measure of growth in Christ, of the share in the divine nature, of the perfection of being attained. The essential joy of heaven is found in the vision of God, and we can appreciate, although we cannot understand, that the perfection of the souls who gaze upon Him must determine the penetration of their gaze and therefore the depth of their joy. God, who rewards all so lavishly, is not less lavish in the reward He gives to those who have merited more. Yet no one is disappointed; each soul receives the reward of which he is capable; each has reached a perfection beyond the dream of man; each is of the company of the blessed, high and low.

It seems to follow from this that a long life on earth is itself a blessing from God, giving as it does greater opportunities for merit, although there are no doubt other factors that affect our merit and it is possible to "redeem the time" in a few short years. However, it is useless for us to inquire into the mystery of God's distribution of graces: He gives freely according to His will, and we cannot search into His ways.

We do know, however, that every grace He gives us brings with it the opportunity of winning fresh graces and greater glory. We can reject His graces or fail to make full use of them, and each opportunity of merit lost is lost forever, so that we should exercise continual vigilance over ourselves in order to husband this precious treasure. In heaven there will be no repining over past failures, but there will be joy in our own perfection, and each grace gained is working out for us an eternal weight of glory.

PART TWO

HEAVEN

With the following chapter, we come to the main subject of this book: heaven itself and its joys. About these, we have quoted more than once the words "No eye has seen, no ear has heard, no human heart conceived the welcome God has prepared for those who love him" (1 Cor. 2:9). These words mean, evidently, that any true understanding or appreciation of the joys of heaven is impossible to us. Yet, on the other hand, we are invited by Holy Scripture to set our thoughts and our hopes above, and we are given not, indeed, a description of heaven but still much information and many hints that provide abundant matter for our meditations. In this and the following chapters we shall attempt to collect and marshal this information.

Since the essential joy of heaven lies in the vision of God and the beatitude that accompanies the vision, we shall devote chapters 5 and 6 to this subject, dealing first with the vision, secondly with the joy the vision gives, for though the two cannot be separated, it is easier for our poor minds to consider them separately. In chapter 7, we return to the vision of God, dwelling especially on the knowledge we shall have of God as Creator. Then we shall in the two following chapters deal with the resurrection of the body and what may be called the lesser joys of heaven. In the last chapter, we shall try to see again what Christ has accomplished in us.

FIVE

The Vision of God

THE blessed shall see God. We know that no man can see God "and live" (Exod. 33:20), that "his dwelling is in unapproachable light; no human eye has seen or can ever see him" (1 Tim. 6:16), and yet the promise that we shall see God is given to us firmly and clearly in Scripture. There are many texts that touch on the question, but two must be quoted that make the promise quite explicitly. The first is from St. Paul's First Letter to the Corinthians, toward the close of his famous hymn to charity: "Our knowledge, our prophesy, are only glimpses of the truth; and these glimpses will be swept away when the time of fulfilment comes.... At present, we are looking at a confused reflection in a mirror; then, we shall see face to face; now, I have only glimpses of knowledge; then I shall recognize God as he has recognized me" (1 Cor. 13:9–12).

Here St. Paul tells us that we shall see and know God, not as now when we see Him through creatures, indirectly as in a mirror, but directly, face-to-face; not obscurely as in a reflection—and it is well to recall that the mirrors he knew were polished pieces of metal, far inferior to ours—but clearly; not partially as glimpses of the truth, but fully. This does not, of course, imply a complete and comprehensive knowledge of God that is and must remain impossible to a finite intellect; it does mean that as God looks directly and immediately into my being, so I shall look on God, no longer as reflected in creatures, no longer with the obscurity of faith, but simply, directly, clearly, immediately in Himself.

The other text to be cited is from the First Letter of St. John where he writes: *"Nunc filii Dei sumus et nondum apparuit quid erimus. Scimus quoniam cum apparuerit similes ei erimus quoniam videbimus eum sicuti est,"* which may be rendered: "We are the sons of God even now, and it has not yet appeared what we shall be. We know that when it does appear, we shall be like to him, since we shall see him as he is" (1 John 3:2; in this passage the rendering from the Latin Vulgate departs from the Knox version, which otherwise is followed throughout this book). These words of St. John, like those of St. Paul, distinguish between our present state and the fulfillment when our knowledge of God will be clear, immediate, and direct: "We shall see him as he is." The words "we shall be like to him" recall St. Paul's "I shall recognize him as he has recognized me," and in St. John the reason why "we shall be like to him" is that "we shall see him as he is." Both writers are in fact attributing to us an intimate knowledge of God of a kind that belongs to God alone, who dwells in unapproachable light.

This, then, has been revealed to us by God, and in revealing it, He invites us to meditate upon it and to try to grasp its substance. In doing so we must encounter difficulties that ultimately are insurmountable: we must not expect to penetrate beyond the limits of the revelation we have received.

Our first difficulty is that we have, even in natural things, no experience of this perfect kind of knowledge, intuition, as it is called—that is, knowing by looking. We do speak of our intuitions, and occasionally we have something approaching true intuition, that is, the direct grasp of a truth, which in a flash is seen in itself and in all its bearings. Ordinarily, however, our knowledge comes to us through reasoning, going from step to step in logical argument, and it may be doubted whether we ever have an intuition properly so-called. To see and, seeing, to know fully and completely, that is not the way our minds work. Yet we have some sort of notion of how an angel seeing, knows—knows without all our train of reasoning. An angel, for instance, seeing a car engine for the first time, would understand at once how it works, more fully even than the designer of the engine, while for one of us, if we have had no previous training, it would take years of work to arrive at a full understanding of the mechanical principles involved in the design. Further, even if we succeed in arriving at some appreciation of what intuition means, we cannot conceive how we could know God in that way. Such knowledge is beyond the natural powers even of the angelic intellect. Yet that is what we are promised: we shall see God, not with our eyes, for He is immaterial; not with our reasoning powers, for that would be obscurely, indirectly; but by intuition, face-to-face, directly. We shall recognize Him as He has recognized us.

To attain to such a knowledge, our minds must of course be strengthened, or more properly not strengthened, for that implies that we have the beginnings of the power already, and we have not, but gifted with a new grace that gives to us an entirely new power, making it possible for men to look on God and live. Theologians call this gift *lumen gloriae*, the light of glory. It is a gift to which a soul, dying in the state of sanctifying grace, has a right, since we are heirs of God, coheirs of Christ, a grace to which God, in creating man, destined him, so that when raised to this share in the divine nature, he yet remains a man, the same man who in anxious fear worked out his salvation in Christ our Lord. It may then be called the fulfillment of what rightly belongs to the adopted children of God.

The second difficulty that we meet in writing of the meaning of this revelation appears equally insurmountable: we shall be trying to express in words what words cannot express, to describe "mysteries which man is not allowed to utter" (2 Cor. 12:4). It seems that at the end we can be no wiser than we were at the beginning; yet the effort must be made, for God invites us to it, and God is there to help us to understand His revelation, in accordance with those words of our Lord: "It is written in the book of the prophets, And they shall have the Lord for their teacher" (John 6:45). This does not mean that our Lord is promising us a new revelation; what He promises is help in discovering the hidden depths of the Faith. Meditation on revealed truth can bring to us a knowledge that before seemed beyond us.

In view of these difficulties, it is important to be quite clear as to what we shall be doing in what follows. We shall be taking the supernatural knowledge that we have by faith from God's revelation of Himself and His Being—known indeed as certain truth, but obscurely—and meditating upon this, we shall be trying to get some faint appreciation of what it means to see God face-to-face and to know these same truths directly and immediately. Beyond this we cannot go, and we should not attempt to do so. We cannot in fact form any true idea of God, or of heaven, beyond the data of revelation, and we should not try to do so, for God Himself has set the limits to His revelation. We shall not then be attempting to learn something new but rather to sound the depths of the riches of the revelation God has already given us. In these depths there is much that will be new to each one of us, for in this life we can never exhaust the riches of the Faith.

We must *meditate*, using our minds but trying to suppress our imaginations. The imagination is fed, as its name implies, on images, on pictures that have come to us through our senses;

we use it rightly when we recall the scenes of our Lord's life, but in representing spiritual ideas it is useless; worse, it is a positive hindrance. Our imagination, for instance, so takes hold of us that we can scarcely prevent ourselves from picturing God outside us, away and apart from us, so that we look at Him as we would look at some scene with human eyes, but God cannot be fitted into any picture, He is not in this place or in that place, He is not large or small; place and time cannot enclose Him. He is not more without us than within us, indeed more within us than without, since He lives His divine life in our souls. Nor, again, in meditating on the Blessed Trinity, must we imagine the three Divine Persons as separate in space. Distinct they are, and yet our Lord says: "I am in the Father, and the Father is in me" (John 14:10), and again we read: "There is no depth in God's nature so deep that the Spirit cannot find it out. Who else can know a man's thoughts, except the man's own spirit that is within him? So no one else can know God's thoughts, but the Spirit of God" (1 Cor. 2:10–11). We have learnt to abandon the effort to picture our own soul present in the body, but the infinite Being of God is immeasurably more outside the scope of our imagination. God's revelation then gives us food for our minds, and it is our minds that we must use in meditating upon heaven.

What then do they see, who see God?

When Moses received the revelation of God from the burning bush, he asked: "What is thy Name?" and God answered him: "I AM." "I am the God who IS." He is Being itself, Existence.

It sometimes happens that a man in this life experiences in a flash well-being in perfect health of mind and body, and in the satisfaction of all his wants, and experiencing this, he exults in his own existence. So, occasionally, we see an animal, a child, a boy, romping with the zest of life. Sometimes, too, when we reflect quite soberly, look into our own consciousness, as it were, stand apart and see ourselves, we are amazed, frightened almost, to find that we exist, that we possess life, that we can feel and think and will. We see at the same time that we might not be, that there was a time when we simply were not, that causes that owed nothing to us combined to give us life, existence; we see that we might not be, and we are aghast. Turning from ourselves to things outside ourselves, to men, to material things, to the earth itself, to the whole universe and all that it contains, we find that they are like us in this: they are, but they might not be. They exist, but their existence requires an explanation. Like us, they could not cause themselves.

If now we follow up the chain of existences that make up the history of the world, we go from one thing that might not be to another that might not be. We come back at last to God, who IS, eternal existence, His own sufficient explanation, the first Cause of all things, Himself uncaused. Nothing has ever existed, but He, Creator of all, has brought it into being. Nothing moves or acts or lives, but He gives it the power to move and act and live. He is the answer to all the questions that have ever been asked. He is the solution to the riddle of the universe. He is the mystery to which men of every age have bowed in awe. God, who is; God the source of being, of life, of all that is good. It is on this that the blessed shall gaze with unblinking eye when they see God, God who was and is and shall be, unchanged, unchangeable.

Gazing on the one true God, the blessed shall see also His intimate and fruitful life. One, as no creature can be one, He is yet three Persons. From the Father there proceeds the only-begotten Son, the uncreated Wisdom of God, the Word of God, the second Person of the Blessed Trinity, distinct as Son from Father, one with the Father in the divine nature. The Son is coeternal, coequal with the Father, in the truest sense Son of the Father "from whom all fatherhood in heaven and on earth takes its title" (Eph. 3:15).

Our experience of persons is confined to human personality—for we do not give the name of person to anything that lacks intellectual powers, to a dog, for instance—and we think of an individual nature as one person. That it can be otherwise we know through faith in God's revelation; how it can be otherwise we cannot know until we see it in God. St. Augustine has given a sort of explanation, founded on revelation: as we conceive an idea, and the thought in our minds is something different from us while yet a part of us, so the Son of God is, as it were, the thought, the wisdom of God, but in God is a distinct Person. However this may be, we know that the divine nature is possessed in two different ways: there are then two Persons, Father and Son.

Father and Son together breathe forth uncreated divine Love, the Breath of God, the Holy Spirit of God, the third Person of the Blessed Trinity, again coeternal with Father and Son, coequal, God, possessing the same individual nature with the Father and the Son. We must not think of this divine life as something completed in the distant past, for as it was in the beginning, so it is now. The blessed in heaven see the eternal divine life: Father begetting Son, Father and Son breathing forth the Holy Spirit.

It was so from the beginning. Then, in time, God, unchanged, decreed to create the world, but He might not have created. Father, Son, and Holy Ghost are sufficient to themselves in eternal beatitude. This thought is too deep for our poor earthly minds. We know that for man, or for any creature, self-complacency is wrong, disorderly; it is so because all that the creature possesses comes to him from God. God, the source of all good, loves perfection, but He finds every perfection in Himself and has no need of anything outside Himself: self-complacency is an attribute of God. The blessed will see this and understand it: one only God, three Persons, not more nor less than three, eternal, necessary, self-sufficient; this they will see and understand, insofar, that is, as created intellect can understand the infinite Godhead. This thought of God alone for all eternity, of His self-sufficiency, frightens us with its implications that He might have remained alone, that we ourselves are nothing in His sight, that we might have remained nothing. Yet for the blessed, there is no terror in this, for they know that He is not alone, that He has called them into being to share His beatitude and His glory, that they are His friends, His children, to whom He wills to show Himself, allowing them to explore the depths of His Divine Being.

I

In what we have been saying, we have been reciting the doctrines of the Creed, the truths revealed by God, seen now with the obscurity of faith, to be seen hereafter openly, unveiled. So we might continue, considering each doctrine separately, but we will limit ourselves to the second great mystery of our Faith, the Incarnation, through which God raises us up to heaven and to a share in His divine life.

First, there is the Person of Jesus Christ, our Lord. The blessed will gaze on this, the greatest work of God, the creation by Father, Son, and Holy Ghost of a complete human nature, body and soul, which at its creation was possessed and made His own by the second Person of the Blessed Trinity. The man, Christ Jesus, in time begins to be, conceived in the womb of the Virgin Mary, to be born and live and die, a man who yet is very God of very God, the only-begotten Son of the Father. Here again, we have the mystery of personality, but now it is one only Person, possessing two natures. True man, He comes as a little child, He adores the Father, prays to Him, does His will, is obedient to Him, offers sacrifice to Him, seeks reward from Him; and yet He is God, one with the Father, united in glory with the Father before the world was, "in whom the whole treasury of wisdom and knowledge is stored up,... the whole plenitude of Deity is embodied" (Col. 2: 3, 9), "a Son, who is the radiance of His Father's splendour, and the full expression of his being" (Heb. 1:3). The blessed will see this human body, like our bodies, yet united with the Word of God, adorable, so that it was the Person of the Word, who was born of the Virgin, who was hungry and tired, who suffered and died. They will see this human soul, like our souls, gifted no doubt with wisdom but with limited human wisdom and not with the infinite wisdom of God, yet the soul of the Word of God, adorable, so that it was the Son of God who was obedient to Joseph and Mary, who was meek and humble of heart, who submitted to His Father's will.

So we might go on, recalling the questions that arise in our hearts when we contemplate the Person of our Savior. Those words and actions of His, recorded in the Gospels, have provided matter for meditation and problems for the learned through the ages; they are pregnant with meaning so that we can never exhaust them, and it is only in the light of heaven that we can hope to fathom "the unfathomable riches of Christ" (Eph. 3:8). Then it will be laid bare to our gaze, for "eternal life is knowing thee, who art the only true God, and Jesus Christ, whom thou hast sent" (John 17:3).

If we turn from the Person of our Lord to consider His work of redemption, we find that we have already received a very full revelation of it, yet at every step we find mysteries that must confound us until the plan is made clear in heaven.

We can understand after some fashion how impossible it was that any mere man should make reparation for our offenses against God's infinite majesty, or merit heaven with the share in the divine nature that is ours. But the plan of God through which we are redeemed, set out so clearly in Holy Scripture, remains so obscure to our minds, tied to earth as they are, that we long for the light that heaven will bring to us when the plan comes to full fruition in each of our souls. I will cite a few of the texts that tell us of the Redemption, to show the unanswered questions that they raise:

Mankind begins with Adam who became, as Scripture tells us, a living soul; it is fulfilled in the Adam who became a life-giving spirit. It was not the principle of spiritual life that came first; natural life came first, then spiritual life; the man who came first came from the earth, fashioned of dust, the man who came afterwards came from heaven, and his fashion is heavenly. The nature of the earth-born man is shared by his earthly sons, the nature of the heaven-born man by his heavenly sons; and it remains for us, who once bore the stamp of earth, to bear the stamp of heaven. (1 Cor. 15:45–49)

There we have a summary of our Lord's work accomplished in us, but the dignity that His coming as man conferred upon our nature, that eludes us. So it is with the means He took to make us "heaven-born." He was a man, with our human nature, and God made Him our head and appointed Him High Priest to approach God on our behalf and make our peace:

We can claim a great high priest, and one who has passed right up through the heavens, Jesus the Son of God. It is not as if our high priest was incapable of feeling for us in our humiliations; he has been through every trial, fashioned as we are, only sinless.... The purpose for which any high priest is chosen from among his fellow men, and made a representative of men in their dealings with God, is to offer gifts and sacrifices in expiation of their sins. (Heb. 4:14–15, 5:1)

We see obscurely in these words how completely our Lord identified Himself with men, that He might make of men the sons of God. The Jewish priests had symbolically placed the sins of the people on the head of the victim to be sacrificed; our High Priest placed them upon His own head: "It is his own blood, not the blood of goats and calves, that has enabled him to enter, once and for all, into the sanctuary; the ransom he has won lasts forever ... and shall not the blood of Christ, who offered himself through the Holy Spirit, as a victim unblemished in God's sight, purify our consciences to serve the living God" (Heb. 9:12–14). He is then victim as well as priest, the Lamb of God, who takes away the sins of the world. All this the blessed will see and understand, and they will see, too, what is so completely hidden from us in this life, the glory of His Passion and death, the victory over evil, the triumph of the Cross, the meaning, too, of that prayer to the Father that He made before His Passion: "Father, the time has come; give glory now to thy Son, that thy Son may give glory to thee. Thou hast put him in authority over all mankind, to bring eternal life to all those thou hast entrusted to him" (John 17:1–2).

This has been set out here at some length because we have reason to think that the full revelation of the Redemption forms an essential part of the joy of the blessed. St. John, in the book of Revelation, which is a vision of heaven, makes this clear. Revelation is concerned very largely with the warfare of God's elect with evil and therefore with Christ's kingdom in this world, but St. John sees "a Lamb, standing upright, yet slain (as I thought) in sacrifice.... And every creature in heaven and on earth and under the earth, and on the sea, and all that is in it, I heard crying out together, Blessing and honour and glory and power, through endless ages, to him who sits on the throne and to the Lamb" (Rev. 5:6, 13). The throne of God is the Lamb's throne; there is no temple or altar in heaven, for the Lamb is temple and altar; there is no sun or moon, for the Lamb is the light thereof.

That the Incarnation of the Son of God and our redemption through Him should occupy a central place in the vision of God that is laid bare to the blessed follows from this that it is Christ our Lord who makes heaven possible to us. He is the foundation of our heaven; He chose to merit for Himself the glory that was His birthright, that He might also merit for us. He came on earth to share with us His divine nature and His Sonship; He has entered heaven the firstborn of many brethren. In Him, then, the blessed will see how they and we are caught up into the life of the Blessed Trinity. God the Father's only-begotten Son in taking human nature achieved the power of giving His divine life to man, so that we live with the life of Christ. Father and Son, breathing forth the Holy Spirit, breathe Him into our souls so that we are temples of God: "To prove that you are sons, God has sent out the Spirit of his Son into your hearts, crying out in us, Abba, Father" (Gal. 4:6). The Holy Spirit dwells in us even on earth, and Christ shares His Sonship with us even on earth, but in heaven we shall see the truth, we shall look on the Blessed Trinity, living the eternal divine life and living it in our souls. Heaven is the home of God, the abode of the Blessed Trinity, and when we enter, we shall know that we belong to heaven, for we, too, are children of God.

SIX

Bliss

W HEN we think of heaven, it is bliss, joy, that is our predomi-
nant thought. Now, in the previous chapter, we have dwelt
almost exclusively on the knowledge that the blessed receive in the
vision of God, although it must be already clear that this vision
yields supreme joy and that it is rightly called the Beatific Vision.
In this chapter we shall try to see why the vision is beatific, and
we are therefore reaching the central idea in our hope of heaven
where we look to find bliss, happiness, delights of every kind, satisfaction of all desires, joy unbounded and pleasure too—in short,
beatitude, though that is rather an ugly name to give to something
so beautiful. It is this, rather than knowledge, that is emphasized
in most of the texts we have quoted, for instance in our Lord's
words: "Your hearts will be glad; and your gladness will be one
which nobody can take away from you" (John 16:22).

We spoke in the previous chapter of God as self-sufficient in
Himself, possessing in Himself every perfection He could desire.
Now the blessed share the life of God; they share, therefore, His
complete beatitude, they possess God, they *enjoy* God. We say they
enjoy God. Now a person can only be enjoyed by union in love

85

with that person. Here in this life we seek to possess the things that attract us and we find satisfaction in their possession. But if it is a person that attracts us, then we love that person; we look for love in return; and we find perhaps our greatest satisfaction and happiness in this life in union with those we love, that is, in friendship. This chapter then is about the love of God, divine charity.

As we shall be speaking of love, of charity, of friendship, we must vindicate the true meaning of these words, for they are often improperly degraded in common speech. Charity, which is sometimes confused with pity or even with less noble sentiments, is used here of the purest love, divine love, for even love of our neighbor if it is charity is part of our love of God. Love itself is essentially benevolence, that is, a wishing well to another; it is not passionate desire, for passionate desire is selfish and true love is essentially unselfish; it is not an emotion, although it commonly gives rise to emotion since, in man, the vigorous activity of the soul reacts upon the body. Mutual love of two persons, with union of mind and will, this is friendship that is not the colorless tolerance that the word is often debased to cover. The meaning our Lord gives to the word *friend*, when He uses it, is the meaning we associate with David and Jonathan, of whom we read: "David's heart was knit to the heart of Jonathan by a close bond, and Jonathan loved David thenceforward as dearly as his own life" (1 Sam. 18:1).

In heaven, then, we shall love God and be loved by Him, and in loving union with Him, our only Good, we shall find happiness. Now, while it is true that we can form no idea of the knowledge that awaits us in heaven, since it is entirely different from the knowledge that we have in this life by faith, the same must not be said of the joy we have by union in love with God. Of this we can have a true foretaste in this life, for even on earth we can be united in love with God. Divine love, charity, on earth or in heaven is one. Charity is the only thing we can take with us from earth to heaven. Faith is for this life only and disappears in the blinding light of heaven; hope falls from us when we enter into possession of that for which we hoped; but "we shall never have finished with charity" (1 Cor. 13:8). Our love of God will blaze out in the next life with our fuller knowledge of Him, for love feeds on knowledge and is nurtured by it, but it is the same love that warms our hearts now and that can inflame them as we grow in that love.

It follows immediately from this that as in the Person of our Divine Lord Himself we receive a revelation of God and of His love, so at the same time we receive a revelation of the joy of heaven that springs from that love. God in His majesty is infinitely far above us, but in Jesus Christ made man we see God; in the beating of His human heart we come to know the love of God: "And the Word was made flesh and came to dwell among us; and we had sight of his glory, glory such as belongs to the Father's only-begotten Son, full of grace and truth.... No man has ever seen God; but now his only-begotten Son, who abides in the bosom of the Father, has himself become our interpreter" (John 1:14–18), and again: "What has revealed the love of God, where we are concerned, is that he has sent his only-begotten Son into the world, so that we might have life through him" (1 John 4:9). Our Lord is our interpreter who teaches us and proves to us the love of God; He is the source of our life, removing the obstacles to our love of God, giving us the grace to love. We know indeed that all that we are comes to us from God; we know that He is Beauty, Truth, that He possesses in infinite degree everything of good that we could desire, but we remain sunk in sin, unable to recognize His love or to love in return, until our Divine Lord, God made man, reveals His love and, elevating us to a share in His own divine life, invites us to a human friendship. For love of us He came into the world, choosing to come as a little infant with all our weakness. Through His life on earth, He did all that man could do to show His love and to win ours. Men, for instance, have been found who sacrificed wealth for a friend; He, Creator and Lord of all things, for love of us despised riches, was born literally by the wayside, lived a life of poverty and want, spent most of His days on earth working as a village carpenter. Some men, a few, have been willing to sacrifice honor for love; He, who had an inalienable right to the worship of all mankind, was pleased for our sake to veil His divinity, to be despised, jeered at, spat upon, mocked. The final test of love, He gives Himself: "This is the greatest love a man can shew, that he should lay down his life for his friends" (John 15:13). For us, then, that we might have life, He died. Death was before His eyes throughout His life, and His love drove Him forward to this inevitable death, foreseen in all its shameful details. In His whole life, and in every mystery of His life, He reveals to us the love of God. We see His patience, His gentleness with sinners, His meekness, His loving heart that yearns for a return of love. That He should be on earth at all is a proof of supreme love, and as we contemplate the details of His life, we learn necessarily the tenderness of His love for us. It is this that explains the transports of joy that the saints experienced in the thought of heaven. Their knowledge of heaven was of the same kind as ours, but the depth of their knowledge of our Lord was not. By meditation on His life and love, they had come to know Him and to love Him. They longed for union with Him, but already on earth, secure in His love, they knew something of the full union of heaven for which they longed. Our Lord had, in this sense, revealed to them the joy of heaven.

As in His Person, so in His words, it is this aspect of heaven that our Lord puts before us most clearly. He does not attempt to describe heaven for us; what He promises is that we shall be united to Him and that we shall share His joy and glory. The kingdom of heaven is a marriage feast in which He is the bridegroom and we the invited guests: "Here is an image, he said, of the kingdom of heaven; there was once a king who held a marriage-feast for his son ..." (Matt. 22:2). He uses this same image on several other occasions, so that it appears to have a special significance, and it is recalled again by St. John in Revelation: "Blessed are those who are bidden to the Lamb's wedding-feast" (Rev. 19:9), where it is the souls of the elect, the Church of Christ, which is the bride of the Lamb.

In other passages, our Lord makes His promise even more personal: we are His friends, our happiness is His concern, He will minister to us Himself. He will say: "Well done, my good and faithful servant;... come and share the joy of thy Lord" (Matt. 25:23), and: "Blessed are those servants whom their master will find watching when he comes; I promise you, he will gird himself, and make them sit down to meat, and minister to them" (Luke 12:37). This promise so full of love is repeated insistently in the discourse after the Supper: He is going to prepare a home for them; He will not leave them orphans; He will see them again and then their hearts will be glad; they will see His glory; they will be united with Him as He with the Father. Finally, in His prayer to the Father after the Supper, the depth of His love and the destiny of His friends is brought out: "I have revealed, and will reveal, thy name to them; so that the love thou hast bestowed upon me may dwell in them, and I, too, may dwell in them" (John 17:26). In this same prayer to the Father, He had claimed for His own human soul the crown of glory that He was to share with us. It was His by right, but He also merited it and showed us how to merit, for His meat had been to do the will of the Father, who sent Him. He was raised up in glory because He had been made obedient to death.

His love was not an empty profession in words but was shown in deeds, and so He would have us to show ours: "If you have any love for me, you must keep the commandments which I give you" (John 14:15). He showed us the love of God, and He showed us how to love God; doing this, He showed us heaven.

I

It is then no accident that the two great texts on the Beatific Vision that we quoted in the previous chapter occur, the one in St. Paul's hymn to charity and the other in a passage where St. John is speaking of divine love, for the apostles learnt thoroughly and preached this lesson of their Master. St. John speaks of himself frequently as "the disciple whom Jesus loved"; this is often interpreted as meaning that St. John was the best-loved disciple, but John himself nowhere makes the claim that he was loved more than the others, and I think that such a claim was far from his thoughts, and that each of the apostles was so overwhelmed with our Lord's personal love that each would have thought of himself as the disciple whom Jesus loved. Though they were all to fail him in the hour of trial, there was no doubt about the love that inspired Peter's cry: "I am ready to lay down my life for thy sake" (John 13:37), or Thomas's: "Let us go too, and be killed along with him" (John 11:16). Living in His company, knowing Him as He was, they could not but love Him. As St. John tells us: "We apostles have seen for ourselves, and can testify, that the Father sent out his Son to be the redeemer of the world, and where a man acknowledges that Jesus is the Son of God, God dwells in him, and he in God; we have learnt to recognize the love God has in our regard, to recognize it, and to make it our belief. God is love; he who dwells in love dwells in God, and God in him" (1 John 4:14–16). Reading the Letters of St. John and his Gospel, we seem at times to breathe the very air of heaven. In their turn, when the apostles went out to preach, they gave the same message of love, and so we find in all the saints this same longing for heaven. Thus St. Paul writes: "Forgetting what I have left behind, intent on what lies before me, I press on with the goal in view, eager for the prize, God's heavenly summons in Christ Jesus" (Phil. 3:13–14). Nowhere perhaps is this love expressed so eloquently as in the famous letter to the Romans of St. Ignatius Martyr, disciple of St. John. He had been condemned to be cast to the beasts in the amphitheater, and fearing that the Christians of Rome might secure his reprieve, he wrote to them:

> I long to enjoy the beasts prepared for me and I pray that they may be swift to bring me to agony and death; ready, too, to devour me, lest, as has happened with other martyrs, they refuse to touch my body. If they do not want to, I will force them, I will strive to be devoured. Forgive me, Children, but I know what is to my advantage. Now, I am beginning to be a disciple of Christ, desiring nothing of this world, that I may find Jesus Christ. Let fire come to me, let the cross, let beasts come, let my bones be broken and my body rent; if only I may enjoy Christ Jesus.

The same fire burns in the equally famous passage of St. Augustine:

> Late have I loved Thee, O Beauty so ancient and so new, late have I loved Thee!... Thou didst breathe fragrance upon me, and I drew in my breath and do now pant for Thee; I have tasted Thee and do now hunger and thirst for Thee. Thou didst touch me and I burned for Thy peace. When once I shall be united with Thee with all my being, there shall be no more grief and toil, and my life shall be alive, filled wholly with Thee.

Such passages might be multiplied almost indefinitely since this love and the longing for heaven that it breeds are found in the lives of every one of the saints. It appears then that we are here close to the secret of that savor of heaven that we seek in this book, and we must pause to examine it more closely.

One might be inclined to think that it was easy for the apostles to love our Lord, seeing that they had personal contact with Him in life, but He Himself said to them after the Supper: "I can say truly that it is better for you that I should go away; he who is to befriend you will not come to you unless I do go, but if only I make my way there, I will send him to you" (John 16:7). The apostles, in their distress at losing Him, could not believe the truth of this statement, but after the Holy Spirit came, they were to prove it by their newfound steadfastness and by their abiding love. Better than the visible presence of our Lord was the indwelling of the Holy Spirit and the growing life of Christ that the Spirit formed in their souls, which in due time He was to form in ours. They, and we too, were to receive not only the gifts of the Holy Spirit but the Holy Spirit Himself: "Do you not understand that you are God's temple, and that God's spirit has his dwelling in you?" (1 Cor. 3:16). Not only that, the Father and Son were to come too: "If a man has any love for me, he will be true to my word; and then he will win my Father's love, and we will both come to him, and make our continual abode with him; whereas the man who has no love for me, lets my sayings pass him by" (John 14:23-24). The intimate life of God, the eternal procession of the three Persons, Father, Son, and Holy Spirit, is present to the soul in grace on earth no less than in heaven. Divine charity is a supernatural gift that comes to us through Christ, for He not only reveals to us the love of God, but He gives it to us, communicating to us His own life.

This then was the source from which the saints drew their love. Such love does not spring from human effort, but it does presuppose human cooperation with the grace of God. The saints knew our Lord, not by reading about Him but by meditating on His life, His life on earth and His life in their own souls, by meditating on Him and by imitating Him, making themselves daily more Christlike. They did not "let his sayings pass them by." Now He is with us as He was with the saints. From our Baptism, He has been present in our souls; when first we learnt to say the Our Father, it was the Spirit of God who made us cry Abba, Father. We have heard about our Lord and His life, His works and words in sermons and instructions. We have read about Him in the Gospels and in books, but from our first prayer, we have been in more intimate contact with Him in our souls; whenever we have turned to Him in prayer, He has been there to listen, to reveal Himself to us, to draw us to Himself. If we have not learned to love Him better, the fault is not His. How often have we been like those lepers who were cleansed and who saddened His heart by their ingratitude when they did not return to thank Him? How often like the rich young man He called to follow Him, who turned away sadly, for he had great riches and he preferred the riches; or like the apostles themselves when He asked them to watch and they slept; or like any of those present at His Passion, who looked on as idle spectators when He was suffering and dying for us? We can have supernatural life without nourishing it; we can forget what we owe to Him, allowing ourselves to be blinded by the world and its cares, having our attention continually distracted from Him. We can let His sayings pass us by, forget the cost of love.

This means that we must be prepared to pay the price of love, as we must pay the price of heaven. He has Himself given us the test: "If you have any love for me, you must keep the command-ments which I give you" (John 14:15), and: "You will live on in my love, if you keep my commandments, just as it is by keeping my Father's commandments that I live on in his love" (John 15:10). This latter text makes it particularly clear that we need seek no more poetic or romantic way of love than keeping the commandments, since it was thus that our Lord in His humanity was made pleasing to the Father. For to keep His commandments is to do His will, to submit our wills to His, to be united with Him in will, and this is to love. Heaven is this union in love with God, but on earth, too, we can be united with Him in everlasting love: we can savor heaven.

It is true, of course, that we cannot perceive this union with God: it does not ordinarily enter into our consciousness, for God wants us to walk here in the obscurity of faith. Love follows knowledge, and only in heaven can we attain to the fullness of knowledge of the glory, the goodness, the beauty of God. There we shall be united, and shall know that we are united, to our supreme Good; we shall be His friends, His children, the members of His household. God is love, and each of the blessed shall see eternal love embracing each personally, for in the eye of God, men are not a confused crowd. Each separate soul is known and loved; each was chosen by eternal decree for creation; to each were given the graces that have led the soul at last to this union with God in heaven. And why? Why did God choose *me* out of the infinite number of men who might have existed and who were not in fact created? Why did I receive all these rich graces? Scripture answers: "That love resides, not in our shewing any love for God, but in his shewing love for us first" (1 John 4:10). That is to say, it was nothing that I deserved or did, since, before I was, He loved me; His love prompted that eternal decree by which I was created; while I was yet sunk in sin, He loved me and sent His Son into the world to redeem me. Again the Scripture tells us: "With unchanging love I love thee, and now in mercy I have drawn thee to myself" (Jer. 31:3). God has drawn each of the blessed in heaven to Himself. Again why? What does God look for in return? Our love, our friendship. He created me because He desired to be loved, and loved by my individual soul. Friendship can only exist between two who have something in common, something of equal dignity. He has, through Jesus Christ, raised me up to share in His divine nature. He has adopted me as His son, that I might enter into His family and be united with Him in eternal friendship. To this, then, in heaven God brings us; we are caught up into the life of the Blessed Trinity. This is the joy of heaven: to know God as I am known: to love God and be loved.

II

We should not be faithful to the teaching of our Lord if we left this subject of charity without mentioning love of our neighbor. The second commandment, "Thou shalt love thy neighbor as thyself," is, He tells us, like to the first, "Thou shalt love the Lord thy God with thy whole heart." It is like to the first because, if we love God, we must love man, who is made in the image and likeness of God, because in one another each of us sees a man for whom Christ died, one destined to be a son of God, a fellow citizen of heaven. Many indeed are unworthy to be called members of Christ, but He died for us all because we were unworthy; we hope to reach heaven not because we have deserved it but because He has deserved it for us. In His description of the last judgment, it is as a reward for charity to our neighbor that our Lord represents the call to enter heaven:

Then the King will say to those who are on his right hand,
Come, you that have received a blessing from my Father,
take possession of the kingdom that has been prepared for
you since the foundation of the world. For I was hungry,
and you gave me food, thirsty, and you gave me drink; I
was a stranger, and you brought me home, naked, and you
clothed me, sick, and you cared for me, a prisoner, and you
came to me. Whereupon the just will answer, Lord, when
was it that we saw thee hungry, and fed thee, or thirsty, and
gave thee drink? When was it that we saw thee a stranger,
and brought thee home, or naked, and clothed thee? When
was it that we saw thee sick or in prison and came to thee?
And the King will answer them, Believe me, when you did
it to one of the least of my brethren here, you did it to me.
(Matt. 25:34-40)

These words, taken together with the condemnation of the damned
because they failed in charity, make clear the central importance
that our Lord attaches to His commandment: "Love one another,
as I have loved you" (John 15:12).

This is a commandment and not a counsel. We are a family,
the children of God; if we are not united in love with His other
children, then we are separating ourselves from the family and
from Him. It is no doubt a difficult commandment that our
Lord has laid upon us, but it is a commandment that we must
keep if we would remain in His love. And if we are completely
honest with ourselves, we shall have to admit that the difficulty
comes not so much from our neighbor who is unlovable as from
ourselves who are too selfish to love. Our neighbor is, perhaps,
uncharitable to us; he even does us injury, or insults us, or worst
of all, ignores us. These things make it hard for us to control our

feelings, but our Lord commands us not to feel love but to show it; our love for our neighbor, like our love for God, is shown by deeds and not by words or feelings. None of us can have such reasons for not loving as our Divine Lord had when, in spite of our sins, of our injuries, our insults, our neglect, He died for us. "Love one another, as I have loved you" is a commandment that in itself disposes of any objections or difficulties we can bring against it.

This practice of charity to our neighbor brings many great advantages to ourselves, but one of these in particular may be noticed here. We must love God if we would save our souls. Do we love God? There are times when we feel doubt about the state of our own consciences, fear about the state of our souls. How can we be sure that we do love God? We cannot be sure of this, but it is not difficult to know whether we love our neighbor, whether we really act toward him in charity. If we do, then we can feel confidence that we love God, too, since it is from our love of Him that we draw our love for our neighbor. This is in effect the sign our Lord gives when He says: "The mark by which all men will know you for my disciples will be the love you bear one another" (John 13:35). This is the sign offered to the world and also to ourselves.

The commandment of our Lord, giving a new meaning to that word, charity, has in fact transformed the world, however blind the unbeliever may be to the transformation. His true disciples do love God, love Jesus Christ whom He has sent, love all men. If all were faithful to His command, as we wrote at the beginning of this book, we should have heaven on earth, and as we shall see in a later chapter, in our heavenly home, this union with our brethren will be an added joy. Our love of our neighbor is in truth directed to heaven. As St. John of the Cross says:

Such is the fervour and power of God's charity that those of whom He takes possession can never again be limited by their own souls or contented with them. Rather it seems to them a small thing to go to heaven alone, wherefore they strive with yearnings and celestial affections and the keenest diligence to take many to heaven with them. This arises from the great love they have for their God and it is the true fruit of perfect prayer and contemplation.

That this is true we see in the lives of many saints who wore themselves out in their zeal for the salvation of souls; it only means, after all, that their love made them like their Master.

Our love for our neighbor, like our love for ourselves, must put first the salvation of the soul, but there are many other things that we need and he needs too, and it is of these that our Lord speaks, enumerating the corporal works of mercy. Certainly a charity that stops at words, even at prayers, making no attempt to relieve the necessities of our neighbor, is cold.

It is evident, however, that our Lord has something else in mind in giving us the commandment and in enumerating the corporal works of mercy. He preached charity; He wants us to preach charity; and the only way to preach charity is by example. We who have received the full revelation of our Lord and His doctrine, who have received such rich graces, are under the obligation of preaching the gospel, of making it known, according to our opportunities, to others. Now the whole gospel is summed up in the two commandments of charity, and we must teach charity to others, as our Lord taught it to us, by practicing it and showing it to them in our lives. His example is ignored or forgotten; it is for His true disciples to reproduce His life in their lives. By this mark will all men know that we are His disciples, and by this they will learn what He came to teach.

"It is fire," He said, "that I have come to spread over the earth, and what better wish can I have than that it should be kindled?" (Luke 12:49). This fire of love brought Him on earth; it drove Him forward to His Passion and death; it inflames the hearts of those who follow Him; it alone can transform the world and bring the souls for whom He died to heaven, which is above all the abode of love.

SEVEN

The Works of God

In the last chapter, we have dwelt on the love of God and on God's desire to be united with us, here and hereafter, in love. Now, if we love God, we shall seek to know Him as fully as we can, and on the other hand, growing to know Him better, we shall come to love Him more. In chapter 5, we dealt with the revelation God has given us of His own life, but we saw also that He is the source of all existence, the first cause of all things. In this chapter we shall consider this more fully and try to see how, in His works, He reveals to us His power and majesty, His beauty and wisdom. The Psalmist sings: "See how the skies proclaim God's glory, how the vault of heaven betrays his craftsmanship" (Ps. 18:2). God's glory is always before our eyes, and we have here matter for meditation for a lifetime, through which we can be growing always in our knowledge and love of God. In the two previous chapters, we have tried in a sense to get a glimpse of heaven, and here we seem to be going back again to the road to heaven: perhaps we are, yet as we said in the beginning of the book, we can only see heaven from this side of the grave, and in studying God's works, as we do here, we are coming closer to an appreciation of what can only be fully revealed to us in heaven. Looking at

God as seen through His material creation, seen especially in man, made to His own image and likeness, and in the workings of His providence, our hearts should be lifted up to Him, Creator of all, who loves us and invites us to His friendship. So we may hope to awaken in ourselves a longing for heaven when we shall gaze on Him and be united to Him.

The skies proclaim God's glory, yet how blind we are to it. Since our insensitiveness to the revelation of the glory of God in His works is parallel to the failure of the agnostic or the atheist to find God at all, we may well begin with the scriptural rebuke to those who are ignorant of God, for the lesson of it we may well take to ourselves. St. Paul, in his Letter to the Romans, says that they are inexcusable who have not known the true God, since His creatures, always before their eyes, reveal Him:

> The knowledge of God is clear to their minds; God himself has made it clear to them: from the foundations of the world men have caught sight of his invisible nature, his eternal power and his divineness, as they are known through his creatures. Thus there is no excuse for them; although they had the knowledge of God, they did not honour him or give thanks to him as God; they became fantastic in their notions, and their senseless hearts grew benighted; they, who claimed to be so wise, turned fools, and exchanged the glory of the imperishable God for representations of perishable man, of bird and beast and reptile. (Rom. 1:19–23)

These words of St. Paul recall an even more striking passage in the book of Wisdom:

> What folly it argues in man's nature, this ignorance of God! So much good seen, and he, who is existent Good, not

known! Should they not learn to recognize the Artificer by the contemplation of his works? Instead, they have pointed us to fire, or wind, or to the nimble air, wheeling stars, or tempestuous waves, or sun and moon, and made gods of them to rule the world! Perhaps the beauty of such things bewitched them into mistaking it for divinity? Ay, but what of him who is Master of them all; what excellence must be his, the Author of all beauty, that could make them! Or was it power, and power's exercise, that awoke their wonderment? Why then, how many times greater must he be, who contrived it! Such great beauty even creatures have, reason is well able to contemplate the Source from which these perfections came. (Wis. 13:1–5)

We see at once the force and truth of this indictment, but surely, if we blame the pagan for worshipping sticks and stones, or the scientist for studying the works of God and failing to find God, we should beware of falling under a like condemnation: the hearts of His children, who have received so full a revelation of Him, should be dilated, when they see His works, at the thought of possessing Him who is the source of so much beauty.

It has often been remarked that men grow so insensible to the marvels of creation that while they are astonished at a miracle, they are indifferent to the daily miracles about them, as the sun rises and sets, or the acorn grows into an oak, or their ear hears the voice of a friend. As St. Paul implies, it is the wise men of the world and the proud, rather than the simple and the humble, who fail to find God; there is a lesson for us here. In our own age, we can see that it is often those who study His works most closely who show the most surprising ignorance of the Creator. Our historians trace the laws of human development and yet are blind to the workings of Providence—blind indeed to the free will of man. One finds a similar failing among men of science, and perhaps for them there is a particular danger that their very preoccupation with the exact measurement of minutia may blind them to the larger view. They are so concerned with secondary causes that they forget the necessity of a first cause. A man will with meticulous care peer through his microscope and work out why a particular seed produces this variety of wheat and not that, or by an ingenious calculation determine why this configuration of electrons results in that effect. Then they are finished; the boundaries of science are enlarged; but why the seed produces wheat at all, who made the seed and the electron, where the world came from, who gave it order, what is the source of matter, of life, of our senses with eye and ear and tongue, how intelligence was born, these questions are forgotten or ignored. What folly it argues in man's nature, this ignorance of God!

It is especially necessary in this age and time that we should remind ourselves that, whatever the wise of this world may think, there are more important things than science. Moreover, we should learn the danger of pride of intellect: a man may be very learned and very humble, but the learned are often proud and the proud look for worshippers rather than for a God to worship. We cannot find God, nor can we know God in His gifts, unless we are humble, unless we know ourselves, that is, for the creatures that we are. There are two ways of using this world and the things that are in it; we may accept them as gifts from God and allow them to lead us to God, or on the other hand, we may regard them as riches within our reach and use them for themselves; then they will cut us off from God. When the gift is a human perfection, like learning, the danger is all the greater. "At that time Jesus said openly, Father, who art Lord of heaven and earth, I give thee praise that thou hast hidden all this from the wise and the prudent, and revealed it to little children. Be it so, Father, since this finds favour in thy sight" (Matt. 11:25–26), and again: "Believe me, unless you become like little children again, you shall not enter the kingdom of heaven" (Matt. 18:3). Our Lord demands that we be as little children when we humbly accept the truths of the Faith; it is as little children that we must look at the wonders of creation. There is a real danger for us of exaltation when we look at the wonderful panorama of what man may be; we are amazed at the beauty that man can conceive and execute in painting, in music, in poetry, in craftsmanship; amazed again at the increasing mastery shown in his control over the forces of nature, his supremacy over the world of matter. Many exult in this and allow it to puff them up. The children of God should rather look to Him who formed it all, who in the world of matter has hidden riches and forces that provide endless occupation for the search of countless generations of men, who made man himself, who is life and giver of life, who can communicate that divine spark that animates man.

I

The first step toward finding God in His creatures is a recognition of the insignificance of man, or ourselves. This majesty, or transcendence, of God is well brought out in chapter 38 of the book of Job and the following chapters. We will quote a portion of chapter 38, where God, as it were, issues a challenge to Job:

> From what vantage-point wast thou watching, when I laid the foundations of the earth? Tell me, whence comes this sure knowledge of thine? Tell me, since thou art so wise, was it thou or I designed earth's plan, measuring it out with the line? How came its base to stand so firm, who

laid its corner-stone? To me, that day, all the morning stars
sang together, all the powers of heaven uttered their joyful
praise. Was it thou or I shut in the sea behind bars? No
sooner had it broken forth from the womb than I dressed
it in swaddling clothes of dark mist, set it within bounds
of my own choosing, made fast with bolt and bar; thus far
thou shalt come, said I, and no further; here let thy swelling
waves spend their force.

Dost thou, a mortal, take command of the day's breaking,
and shew the dawn its appointed post, twitching away earth's
coverlet, scaring away the ill-doers? The dawn, that stamps
its image on the clay of earth, stands there, flung over it like
a garment, taking away from the ill-doers the darkness that
is their light, so that all their power goes for nothing. Didst
thou ever make thy way into the sea's depths, walk at thy ease
through its hidden caverns? When did the gates of death
open to thee, and give thee sight of its gloomy threshold? Nay,
hast thou viewed the whole surface of the earth itself? Tell
me, if such knowledge is thine, all its secrets; where the light
dwells, where darkness finds its home; hast thou followed
either of these to the end of its journey, tracked it to its lair?
Didst thou foresee the time of thy own birth, couldst thou
foretell the years of life that lay before thee? (Job 38:4–21)

And thus Job answered the Lord: "I acknowledge it, thou canst
do all thou wilt, and no thought is too difficult for thee" (Job
42:1–2). The order, the beauty, the life in the world, the justice,
the mercy, the holiness we find in men, should make us think of
power, beauty, holiness subsistent in the eternal God, Creator of
all. Since His works are always before us, our minds should be
constantly lifted by them to God.

Who is like to God? There is in this world nothing that can give us a true idea of God: as we said in a previous chapter, so here we must recall that our imagination with its sense images is rather a hindrance than a help. We arrive at some knowledge of God and His nature, first, in a purely negative way by realizing that any imperfections, limitations, or blemishes that we see in creatures are wholly absent in Him, but secondly, and in a more positive way, by turning to the subsistent perfection that is God's from the limited perfection that we find in creatures. If, for instance, we find beauty so marvelous as to make us gasp with awe yet limited as created beauty must be, to think of Him as beauty without limit, beauty subsistent. This is the method used in that passage we have quoted from the book of Wisdom: "Perhaps the beauty of such things bewitched them into mistaking it for divinity? Ay, but what of him who is Master of them all; what excellence must be his, the Author of all beauty, that could make them!"

Everything we see is material, but He is pure Spirit; material things are complex, made up of parts, and, being complex, are subject to change and to decay. He is pure, simple, receiving nothing from another, even so much as an angel who also is pure spirit but who receives from God being, existence, life. We have spoken of God as simple, and we have said also that He is subsistent Beauty; the two really convey the same notion in different ways. It is not that He is beautiful, wise; no, He is Beauty, He is Wisdom—as St. Augustine expresses it, what He has, that He is. This is an idea we cannot fathom, but it is well, before we go on to speak of God's attributes, that we should make the effort to see where our human minds are introducing limitations and imperfections into the conception we form of God.

We speak of God as being pleased or angry, but He is unchangeable: "The Father of all that gives light, with whom there can be no change, no swerving from his course" (James 1:17). All that we see takes place in time, but He is eternal, which means not merely that He had no beginning. This indeed, but much more, that He is outside time, so that all time lies before Him in an eternal present: "I am Alpha, I am Omega, the beginning of all things and their end, says the Lord God; he who is, and ever was, and is still to come, the Almighty" (Rev. 1:8). We say that He is present everywhere, but again it is more than this, for everything that exists depends upon Him so that His power is operating everywhere. He created all, but His creatures are kept in being only by His continuing creative will: "All creation depends for its support on his enabling word" (Heb. 1:3). His presence we find a check upon our waywardness, but also an encouragement in our efforts: we are always in His sight: "From him, no creature can be hidden; everything lies bare, everything is brought face to face with him, this God to whom we must give our account" (Heb. 4:13). All things are present to Him who is the cause of all. If we read, for instance, the twenty-first Psalm, we seem to be reading a historical poem on the Passion, as in the verse "they divide my spoils among them, cast lots for my clothing" or "they have torn holes in my hands and my feet; I can count my bones one by one." Yet this psalm was written more than a thousand years before the Passion of our Lord. So the priests, relying on a seven-hundred-year-old prophecy, were able, without hesitation, to tell Herod that Christ was to be born in Bethlehem. Again, it was the decree for the enrollment of the world, made by Caesar Augustus, unconscious as he was of God's purposes, that in God's providence ensured the fulfillment of this prophecy. The man born blind was born blind that Jesus might cure him, "that God's action might declare itself in him" (John 9:3). His wisdom by which He disposes all things sweetly, His power that reaches from end to end, His justice, giving to each his due, His mercy, which tempers His justice, these continually direct His action in the world. Yet men dare to query His wisdom, "Why did God allow the war?"; His justice, "Why has God done this to me?"; His mercy, "Thou art a hard master, that reaps where he did not sow." Our little minds should know this at least, that they cannot pit themselves against His infinite majesty: "What, wouldst thou search out the ways of God, have knowledge unconfined of his omnipotence; high as heaven is that wisdom and thy reach so small; deep as hell itself, and thy thought so shallow" (Job 11:7–8). We must remember that we are little children.

Of his mercy, the world is full: "How pitying and gracious the Lord is, how patient, how rich in mercy; he will not always be finding fault, his frown does not last for ever; he does not treat us as our sins deserve, does not exact the penalty of our wrongdoing. High as heaven above the earth towers his mercy for the men that fear him; far as the east is from the west, he clears away our guilt from us" (Ps. 102:8–12). His holiness demands that with mercy shall go justice: "So just, Lord, thou art, thy awards so truly given! Strict justice and utter faithfulness inspire all thy decrees" (Ps. 118:137–138). It brings out very well the limitations of our thought that we think of God as now just, now merciful, but He is always both the one and the other: in every act, most just, in the same act, most merciful: "No award of thine but is deserved, no act of thine but tells of mercy, of faithfulness, and of justice" (Tob. 3:2).

His wisdom and power, His knowledge and providence, His mercy and justice are always before our eyes, and our whole lives can be a meditation on His perfections. He made all things, and He saw that all He made was good; everything is ordered, controlled, instinct with the spirit of beauty. The material universe, with its thousand light-years as a measure of distance, is a thing quite simple, matter-of-fact, material, and yet our puny minds boggle at it. The stars and universes of stars hang in the heavens while man slowly fathoms their depths and shrinks before Him, who, with a word, called them into being. We turn from these immensities and look through a microscope at, say, a slide of the inflorescence of a daisy, and our breath is taken away by an incredible new beauty, new order, invisible to the human eye. An ordinary oak tree may have on it some three million leaves, all alike, yet individual, each varying a little from the common pattern, each known and formed by God. What of the number of leaves He has formed in the life of this tree, of all trees, the number He forms each year, each century? "See how the lilies grow; they do not toil or spin, and yet I tell you that even Solomon in all his glory was not arrayed like one of these" (Luke 12:27). If we go into one of these aquariums, where fish can be seen swimming in their natural surroundings, we find marvels of form, of color, of quaintness; even in fish brought up from the depths of the sea, never perhaps before seen by man, there is the same inexhaustible richness of all creation. In plant and animal, in the minerals of the earth, awaiting man's needs, in sea and air and sky, God lavishes His gifts upon us. The message He would have us read in them is this: Power, Beauty, Wisdom; God, before whom we are nothing, is waiting upon us, seeking to raise us up to Himself, to give Himself to us, to unite us with Himself in eternal love.

II

Now, let us consider for a moment His providence. We speak of the chances and accidents of life, but there is no chance, no accident, for all is ruled by His governing plan: "Looking down from heaven, he watches all mankind, his immovable dwelling has the whole world in view; he has fashioned each man's nature, and weighs the actions of each" (Ps. 32:13-15), and "In heaven and on earth, in the sea and in the deep waters beneath us, the Lord accomplishes his will" (Ps. 134:6). They tell us that with every breath we draw, every mouthful of food we eat, germs innumerable enter our bodies; they are known, every one, and are in the directing hand of God. Every breath, every heartbeat, He counts. "He takes every hair of your head into his reckoning" (Matt. 10:30). The friends about us, our disappointments, our successes, all come from God. Our sins alone are our own, but even on these His providence at once seizes, that He may exercise that divine prerogative of bringing good out of evil so that our falls and our waywardness will be remembered in heaven only by the greater glory that through them and His great mercy we have attained—much as the sins of Mary Magdalene are remembered by us.

Our Lord said to the apostles: "I am here among you as your servant" (Luke 22:27), and God seems to make Himself our servant as He works continually for our good, guiding by His providence the circumstances of our lives, seeking always to draw us to Himself. We see a landscape that transports us with its majesty; God made it for that purpose. We look, say, into a tropical jungle and, in the teeming life of one square yard, we see a lifetime of scientific work, if we would give ourselves to unravelling it; God placed it there to excite our humble wonder. We are laid low by sickness and find perhaps that through it we come to know our weakness and are forced to look to Him for strength. For even here in this life, we sometimes see that a great affliction or a disappointment in some undertaking that comes, it may be after fervent prayers, was a blessing beyond our dreams. So a man has told me that a long internment in an enemy prison camp was the greatest grace he had received in his life. We can only cry with St. Paul: "How deep is the mine of God's wisdom, of his knowledge; how inscrutable are his judgements, how undiscoverable his ways! Who has ever understood the Lord's thoughts, or been his counsellor? Who ever was the first to give, and so earned his favours? All things find in him their origin, their impulse, the centre of their being; to him be glory throughout all ages, Amen" (Rom. 11:33–36). This is the God who seeks to receive us into His household!

In what we have said above, there is little about man, but man, made in the image of God, is the greatest of God's works. Our lives are passed among men and their works, and from them we can learn much of God. Looking at the works of man, nothing stirs us so much as his great and heroic exploits, but we have not time here to dwell on these. We will make mention only of what we must recognize, unless our minds are warped by worldliness as the highest of human achievements, the holy life of the saint. There is here, if we are not blind to it, a revelation of the holiness of God. The life of a St. Francis of Assisi, full of love of creatures and of their Creator, of simplicity, of heavenly wisdom, moves even men who do not realize whence that stream flows. A St. Vincent de Paul, although he died three hundred years ago, still lives on earth in his beneficent influence, giving his name and his inspiration to so many works of charity, because he possessed the spirit of his Master. What a rich variety there is in God's saints: the singleness of purpose of a St. Agnes or a St. Francis Xavier, the steadfastness of Joan of Arc or Thomas More, the learning of Thomas Aquinas or the love of Margaret Mary, Augustine, or Catherine of Siena! Of our Blessed Lady, Queen of them all, Queen of heaven, we must speak later, but here we pause to see her as the greatest of God's creatures in her surpassing holiness, her purity, her fruitful virginal womb, her mother's love that embraces each of her children, knows every one of each child's needs; a model for us all since she comes closest to God; a Mother for us all since she most nearly imitates the all-embracing love of God; beautiful beyond words with the beauty of God. She, too, is a gift from the riches of God: "Whatever gifts are worth having, whatever endowments are perfect of their kind, these come down to us from above; they are sent down by the Father of all that gives light, with whom there can be no change, no swerving from his course; and it was his will to give us birth, through his true word, meaning us to be the first-fruits, as it were, of all his creation" (James 1:17–18). Holiness, humility, wisdom, charity, love, all these we find in men and women, and this blossoming of our human nature elevates our hearts to the source whence all this flows. These are but sparks lit from the furnace of love and wisdom and holiness.

III

With these thoughts, we have been trying to build upon the beauty and power and love that are with us even now in order to reach out toward the knowledge that the vision of God will bring to us, when through eternity we are occupied with the search into the infinite riches of His Being. It is noteworthy that, in the texts that promise us heaven, what is held out to us constantly is not simply joy or happiness but *glory*. Not the satisfaction of human aspirations but a share in the splendor of the majesty of God is to be the portion of His children.

Dante, in his *Paradiso*, describes how the blessed in heaven can read all things, even one another's thoughts, in the vision of God. God is the universal cause of all things, and therefore, in His essence, all things can be seen, all that is good, all that He has accomplished. They will see the birth of the world, its gradual formation by His creative power, the strange creatures that have occupied it, the ages that prepared it for man, that evolution of living things on which man sometimes indulges in the most fantastic speculation; the coming of Adam and Eve, living the life for which our Creator destined us, free, happy, immortal; man's sin that wrecked this plan and God's new plan that made of Adam's sin a *felix culpa,* a happy fault, since it merited so great a Redeemer; the course of the world's history, even the diverse lines of descent from Adam, traced down to each individual birth; the Jewish people and their checkered record; the preparation for Christ's coming, the Annunciation, the Nativity at Bethlehem, the mystery of His life on earth and of the sanctification of the world; His death and the final triumph of sin, which was in His providence the final defeat of sin by the folly of the Cross — the story, summed up in the words: "But what we preach is Christ crucified; to the Jews a discouragement, to the Gentiles, mere folly; but to us who have been called, Jew and Gentile alike, Christ the power of God, Christ the wisdom of God. So much wiser than men is God's foolishness; so much stronger than men is God's weakness" (1 Cor. 1:23–25). What a revelation we are to receive when we can look into the ways of God!

The blessed will see the economy of the Redemption, how Christ our Lord communicates His life to His faithful followers and makes of mere men true children of God, with the likeness of their Father in their souls. They can trace out the progress of His gospel through the ages, where again and again the weakness of Christ confounds the strong; they will see kingdoms rise and fall, evil triumph and wither away before the Church of Christ; they will see the abiding strength of Christ in His members, and His Mystical Body growing, ever growing, to perfect stature and to full manhood up to the end of time.

Even in this, as we make a wide sweep over the working of God's providence, we are conscious of how very human a view we are taking; we can have no inkling of what the vision will reveal to us. Consider, for instance, these words of our Lord: "So it is, I tell you, with the angels of God; there is joy among them over one sinner that repents" (Luke 15:10). For the angels, then, and for the blessed, there are no vague outlines of some master plan that governs mankind in the mass, but Providence working in the individual soul of every man who has ever lived on earth, guiding, directing, governing every moment of each soul's life; every moment of each soul's life gives to the blessed a revelation of the mercy and goodness and wisdom of God.

Each one of us, no doubt, will find a special joy in his own life, seeing the way prepared for it through the ages, as God guided every influence that should bring each of us into being and mold us when we should be born: our parents and whence they derived the Faith, our family, our birth, every detail of our life; especially every detail of our supernatural life from our Baptism through every hourly grace, through terrible dangers that we never knew, but from which our guardian angel and our Blessed Mother protected us; through little steps that seemed negligible but were fraught with eternal consequences; our merits building up continually our life in Christ until we were ripe for home, for heaven.

EIGHT

The Resurrection of the Body

I<small>F</small> we had had our reason alone to guide us, we should still have been inclined to suspect that our souls were immortal. Although we could not have foreseen an eternal existence, yet we would know that the soul is of its nature free from the seeds of decay, and therefore it would appear that God, who made it so, would not withdraw His sustaining hand. With the body, it is quite otherwise, for it is material and visibly subject to decay and to such decay as gives us no inkling that it could be revivified. Some pagans have had myths of bodies transferred to heaven, but they are myths that bear all the marks of irrational legend. It is then only through revelation that we know that our bodies are destined to rise again, but on this truth, revelation is emphatic. It is taught over and over again in Holy Scripture: "I know that my Redeemer liveth and on the last day I shall rise and shall be clothed with my skin and in my flesh I shall see God" (Job 19:25–26). These words are used in the burial service, and we can take them as the teaching of the Church, but in the original text they are of doubtful meaning.

There are, however, many passages in the New Testament that place the teaching of Scripture beyond doubt; thus, "Martha said to him: I know well enough that he will rise again at the resurrection when the last day comes. Jesus said to her, I am the resurrection and life; he who believes in me, though he is dead, will live on; and whoever has life, and has faith in me, to all eternity cannot die" (John 11:24-26). Here our Lord is speaking to Martha about the resurrection of her brother Lazarus, and we may take the subsequent resuscitation of Lazarus as a proof of our Lord's greater promise of eternal life. Speaking of the Eucharist, He had said: "The man who eats my flesh and drinks my blood enjoys eternal life, and I will raise him up at the last day" (John 6:55). Elsewhere, our Lord makes it clear that the resurrection of the body is promised to good and bad alike, to the former as reward, to the latter for punishment: "If thy right eye is the occasion of thy falling into sin, pluck it out and cast it away from thee; better to lose one part of thy body than to have the whole cast into hell" (Matt. 5:29), and still more explicitly in the text: "The time is coming, when all those who are in their graves will hear his voice and will come out of them; those whose actions have been good, rising to new life, and those whose doings have been evil, rising to meet their sentence" (John 5:28-29).

The doctrine of the resurrection of the body is mentioned in the Creeds, and there seems to have been more emphasis placed on it in the early Church than we are accustomed to give to it. St. Paul mentions it constantly in his teaching, for example, to the Athenians and to Felix (Acts 17:18, 32; Acts 24:15). In his Letters to the Corinthians and to the Thessalonians, he mentions his earlier teaching on the subject, and we get the impression that it formed part of his elementary catechetics. Since every early instruction would rest on the proof of our Lord's Resurrection, it would be altogether natural that mention should be made of our own resurrection. In his first Epistle to the Corinthians, St. Paul has to deal with an early heresy that called in question the fact of our bodily resurrection, and in chapter 15, he proves the doctrine, first from our Lord's Resurrection, secondly from the efficacy of the Redemption, and thirdly from our own work and labor, which find in it reward, and he goes on to refute the objections that have been raised against it.

That we should make less of the doctrine is strange, but perhaps we have been unduly influenced by some ascetical writers who from a long tradition, not without some basis in Scripture, have been accustomed to belittle and blame the body. Our Lord Himself says: "The spirit is willing enough, but the flesh is weak" (Matt. 26:41), and St. Paul: "Let me say this; learn to live and move in the spirit; then there is no danger of your giving way to the impulses of corrupt nature. The impulses of nature and the impulses of the spirit are at war with one another; either is clean contrary to the other, and that is why you cannot do all that your will approves" (Gal. 5:16–17). The word that the Knox version here translates as *nature* is in the Douay version *flesh*, and the condemnation of the body, sometimes exaggerated by ascetical writers, arises perhaps from the confusion that identifies the flesh with the body, whereas in Holy Scripture, and especially in St. Paul, the meaning is rather *"corrupt nature"* unregenerated by grace. St. Paul elsewhere speaks of the body as holy, a temple of God, and we must be careful when we speak of "the world, the flesh and the devil" to note that the flesh does not mean the body, but corrupt nature, as St. Paul speaks of it. We are apt to think of concupiscence and the effects of original sin as residing in the body, but the effects are in the soul too. If the soul complains of being burdened, led into sin by the body, which refuses to follow its high aspirations and drags it in the mire, the body, if it could speak up for itself, might well answer that it has not noticed these high aspirations, that it is the sluggish inertia of the soul that holds it back from higher things, that if the soul does make any sacrifice, it is the body that pays the price, that if it falls into sin, it is the soul, the will, that sins.

All this, however, exaggerates the separation of soul and body. Man is a composite being, made up of two parts that are unlike, even opposed, but that yet form a single being: man is *one*. The body is not a suit of clothes, however well-fitting; the soul is not burdened, imprisoned; it is indwelling in the body, forming with it one person, giving it life—the only life we know. So true is this that we cannot imagine nor conceive what life will be when the soul has left the body, but we know that it will not be, in the full sense, the life of a man. God has made man, body and soul; our service of Him is the service of the whole man, and He designs to reward us wholly, raising up body and soul. Before the last judgment, it is true, the soul will be without its body, and it will then be in a real sense incomplete, for the soul was designed and created to inform a body. The death and decay of the body, and its temporary separation from the soul, are a consequence of sin, and Pope Pius XII, in his definition of the Assumption of our Blessed Lady, says that the Assumption follows connaturally on her Immaculate Conception: her body did not see corruption, because she had never known sin.

How could we think that there is anything evil, anything unworthy even, in the human body when we remember that our Divine Lord took a human body and soul and united them to the second Person of the Blessed Trinity in the Incarnation. It was necessary for the plan of the Redemption that He should take a body and soul, for in doing so, He took to Himself mortality, that He might redeem us by His death. In the Eucharist, He has given us His Body as food, food, we say, for our souls, but we receive His Body into our bodies, and He Himself insists that this is the sacrament of our resurrection: "The man who eats my flesh and drinks my blood enjoys eternal life, and

I will raise him up at the last day" (John 6:55). His body, too, is the mystical symbol of that Body of His that is the Church, to which He gives life here on earth, which is growing to perfect stature and which, as we shall see in a later chapter, finds its consummation in heaven.

We need not dwell on the practical difficulty of gathering up the fragments of the men who have peopled the earth, with so many bodies formed from a limited amount of material; some of the attempts that have been made to solve this problem read like suggestions offered to God from the height of our scientific knowledge. It is in fact extraordinary how little we know of the nature and the constitution of matter. Science, which has made such amazing advances in technology, in the control and utilization of material forces, is still groping when it attempts to interpret its own results; the particles it has to deal with are so excessively minute as to baffle all efforts to explore their constitution. St. Augustine mentions the difficulty raised by cannibalism where a man's body is actually eaten by other men and becomes assimilated into their bodies. His conclusion is that God has told us that we shall receive our bodies again—and it will be the same body, not another, just as good—and this should be enough for us. God has promised it; it is not beyond His power; we should leave the details to God. St. Augustine also discusses the kind of body we shall have, considering those who have died in infancy or who are crippled or deformed. He is of the opinion, but here it is only a matter of opinion, that the body will rise at perfect maturity—which he puts between the age of thirty and forty—and perfect in form.[1] Yet we think of our Lord's body as still bearing the marks of His wounds, and one

---

[1] Origen also held that the body would rise perfect in form, but he added that the sphere is the perfect form and concluded that the body would rise spherical! This opinion has been condemned by the Church.

would think that the martyrs, too, will not be without the signs of those wounds that, once so painful, would now be their glory, but here again we are in the region of speculation.

Clearly, our only reliable information must come from Holy Scripture, and St. Paul does deal with this question of the nature of the risen body:

> But perhaps someone will ask, How can the dead rise up?
> What kind of body will they be wearing when they appear?
> Poor fool, when thou sowest seed in the ground, it must
> die before it can be brought to life; and what thou sowest
> is not the full body that is one day to be, it is only the bare
> grain, of wheat, it may be, or some other crop; it is for
> God to embody it according to his will, each grain in the
> body that belongs to it.... The sun has its own beauty, the
> moon has hers, the stars have theirs, one star even differs
> from another in its beauty. So it is with the resurrection
> of the dead. What is sown corruptible, rises incorruptible;
> what is sown unhonoured, rises in glory; what is sown in
> weakness, is raised in power; what is sown a natural body,
> rises a spiritual body.... It will happen in a moment, in
> the twinkling of an eye, when the last trumpet sounds; the
> trumpet will sound, and the dead will rise again, free from
> corruption, and we shall find ourselves changed; this cor-
> ruptible nature of ours must be clothed with incorruptible
> life, this mortal nature with immortality. Then, when this
> corruptible nature wears its incorruptible garment, this
> mortal nature its immortality, the saying of Scripture will
> come true, Death is swallowed up in victory ... thanks be
> to God, then, who gives us victory through our Lord Jesus
> Christ. (1 Cor. 15)

This passage tells us something of what awaits us. The simile of the plant and the seed is most illuminating with its suggestion that the material body, as we know it, is designed by God for elevation and is capable of a perfection that as yet we do not know. We should have been inclined to think that corruptibility is of the essence of matter, subject as it is to change and therefore to decay, and we think of matter as the very opposite of spiritual, for to us spiritual means immaterial. But the word *immaterial* expresses a purely negative idea and therefore must not be taken as the correct definition of spiritual. We really do not know how far matter is capable of being spiritualized, of taking on incorruptibility, without essential change in its nature. It is a chastening thought when we try to picture heaven that in this, which is something quite close to our understanding, we must confess that "no eye has seen, no ear has heard." We have St. Paul's assurance that we shall be greatly changed in heaven; our bodies will be transformed, immortal, spiritualized, incorruptible, incapable of suffering. On the other hand, we know also that changed as we shall be in body and soul, it will yet be I, the same individual who served God in this life, who will receive the reward in the next: it will be the same body and the same soul that receives glory. Were it otherwise, the promise of reward that our Lord gives us would be meaningless.

Of the properties of the risen body, we can get some hint from the appearance of our Lord's body in the Resurrection. The apostles were slow to believe in this wonderful miracle, having seen His dead body laid in the tomb. They had convinced themselves that the tomb was empty, but their final doubts were only dispelled by the force of the facts when they saw Him there amongst them, alive, exactly as they had known Him before but with the wounds still in His hands and feet and side; and yet His body was changed. He appeared suddenly in the supper chamber, the doors being closed. He walked with the disciples to Emmaus and suddenly disappeared from their sight. The body seems to have that mobility that we conceive a spirit, such as an angel, to have, going instantly from one place to another, passing through closed doors. Yet he allowed the apostles to see and handle His wounds; He sat down at table and ate "a piece of roast fish and a honeycomb." His eating was no doubt not a sign that He needed food, but rather a demonstration to them of the reality of His body; for He had to argue with them: "Look at my hands and my feet, to be assured that it is myself; touch me, and look; a spirit has not flesh and bones as you see that I have.... Have you anything here to eat?" (Luke 24:31, 39–41). Slow as they were to believe, the evidence of their senses made doubt impossible, and they were confirmed in that faith that was to be the basis of their teaching when they set out to convert the world. One thing our Lord did not allow them to see in His risen body and that is the glory that of right belonged to it: some of them had seen this in the Transfiguration, but apart from that it was hidden from mortal men.

The Resurrection of our Lord is an exemplar and, at the same time, a pledge of our own resurrection. Our Lord's body was like our bodies, and He had conquered death not only in His own body but in ours also: "Christ has risen from the dead, the first-fruits of all those who have fallen asleep; a man had brought us death, and a man should bring us resurrection from the dead; just as all have died with Adam, so with Christ all will be brought to life. But each must rise in his own rank; Christ is the first-fruits, and after him follow those who belong to him, those who have put their trust in his return" (1 Cor. 15:20–23). So much for the pledge; as to the form of the risen body, "he will form this humbled body of ours anew, moulding it into the image of his glorified body, so effective is his power to make all things obey him" (Phil. 3:21). The apostles, then, who had been so completely broken when our Lord died on the Cross, found peace in the Resurrection and, most surprisingly, were overjoyed at the Ascension when He finally departed from them: "Even as he blessed them he parted from them, and was carried up into heaven. So they bowed down to worship him, and went back full of joy to Jerusalem" (Luke 24:51–52). They were full of joy, for He had gone to prepare a place for them, the firstborn of many brethren. As He had risen, they would rise; as He had ascended into heaven, they, too, would ascend.

Some few years later, our Blessed Lady, His Immaculate Mother, joined Him, body and soul, in heaven and there reigns with Him, waiting to receive us into her court. In bestowing this privilege upon His Mother, our Lord shows us how estimable a thing it is and what added joy and glory there will be for us, too, in the possession of our risen bodies.

I

Is heaven a *place*? That it is a *state* is clear enough: our guardian angel, if he is at our side, does not thereby cease to be in heaven. The thought of the bodily resurrection of our Lord and His Blessed Mother, and of our own future resurrection, urges this question upon us: Is heaven a definite place, and, if so, where is it? The risen body, no doubt, has something of the properties of a spirit, but one would think that normally it must be in some place. We are accustomed to think of heaven as somewhere up in the sky, and in this we have the sanction of our Lord Himself, for when He prayed in public as at the raising of Lazarus (John 11:41) or after the Last Supper (John 17:1), we are told that "he raised his eyes to heaven." At the Ascension, He was "lifted up, and a cloud caught him away from their sight" (Acts 1:9). We can scarcely take these passages as definite teaching on the subject, yet they do confirm the common feeling. Perhaps Dante, who places his heaven in the celestial spheres of the old astronomy, was not so very far from the truth after all. It is very remarkable that we seem to have no theory at all to account for the immensity of this universe that modern astronomy reveals to us. What is God's purpose in this vast creation, in which this earth is such a minute speck? Of the central importance of the earth, we can have no doubt, and this is not because we are, as some have said, attaching undue importance to man. We know the importance of this earth from the fact that it has seen the Incarnation, the life and death of the Son of God. We can have little doubt that the rest of the universe was made for the sake of the earth and its inhabitants, but how or why, we do not know.

It would seem to follow from the resurrection of men's material bodies that there will be a material paradise to receive them, and, in fact, the promise that there will be "a new heaven and a new earth" is repeated several times in Scripture, in the prophesy of Isaiah (Isa. 65:17) and in the Revelation of St. John (Rev. 21:1). St. Peter is quite definite: "But the day of the Lord is coming, and when it comes it will be upon you like a thief. The heavens will vanish in a whirlwind, the elements will be scorched up and dissolve, earth, and all earth's achievements, will burn away.... And meanwhile, we have new heavens and a new earth to look forward to, the dwelling place of holiness; that is what he has promised" (2 Pet. 3:10, 13). It is difficult, in interpreting such passages in Scripture, to say how far they are to be taken in a literal sense, and how far they condescend to our imaginations, as our Lord does in the image of the marriage feast. Nevertheless, the oft-repeated promise of a new heaven and a new earth seems clear and explicit. Further, Holy Scripture seems to indicate that it is not to be so much a new creation as a renewal, a re-creation, of the old: "Behold I make all things new" (Rev. 21:5). All things will be renewed in Christ.

II

Arising out of this, there is a curious error in a number of early Christian writers, which found in this promise the hope of a sensual paradise, very earthly, not to say earthy, such as is promised to the Muslim faithful. These Christian writers were led astray by such words as "I allot to you a place to eat and drink at my table in my kingdom" (Luke 22:29–30), by the parable of the marriage feast, and by a passage in Revelation that speaks of Christ reigning for a thousand years. This passage refers almost certainly to the Christian era, to the time that is to elapse between the Ascension and the second coming of Christ. Consequently, the Fathers of the Church, St. Jerome, St. Augustine, and others firmly condemn this idea of an earthly paradise. After all, we are striving at our Lord's command to detach ourselves from the pleasures of the senses even on earth; we know that they are unworthy of man, that attachment to them endangers our eternal salvation and makes us incapable of savoring the joy of heaven. Man was made for higher things, and even in this world the slave of his senses is despised. St. Augustine, in *The City of God*, says that these sensual pleasures, eating, drinking, and the like, are the pleasures of sickness rather than of health. St. Thomas More, seemingly inspired by this passage in St. Augustine, repeats his condemnation in his racy way:

> Wherefore, in the meantime, for lack of such experimental taste, as God giveth here sometime to some of His special servants to the intent we may draw toward the spiritual exercise too, for which spiritual exercise God with that gift as with an earnest penny of their whole

reward after in heaven comforteth them here on earth, let us not so much with looking to have described what manner of joys they shall be as with hearing what our Lord telleth us in Holy Scripture how marvellous great they shall be, labour by prayer to conceive in our hearts such a fervent longing for them, that we may for attaining to them utterly set at naught all fleshly delight, all worldly pleasures, all earthly losses, all bodily torment and pain. Howbeit, some things are there in Scripture expressed of the pleasures and joys that we shall have in heaven, as where *Fulgebunt iusti sicut sol, et qui erudiunt ad iustitiam, tamquam scintillæ in arundineto discurrunt*: Righteous men shall shine as the sun, and shall run about like sparkles of fire among reeds.

Now tell some carnal-minded man of this manner pleasure, and he shall take little pleasure therein and say he careth not to have his flesh shine, he, nor like a spark of fire to skip about in the sky. Tell him that his body shall be impassable and never feel harm. Yet if he think then therewith, that he shall never be an-hungered nor athirst, and shall thereby forbear all his pleasure of eating and drinking; and that he shall never have list to sleep, and thereby lose the pleasure that he was wont to take in slugging; and that men and women shall there live together without any manner mind or motion unto the carnal act of generation, and that he shall thereby not use there his old filthy voluptuous fashion; he will say he is better at ease already and would not give this world for that. For, as St. Paul saith: *Animalis homo non percipit ea quae sunt spiritus Dei. Stultitia enim est illi*: a carnal man feeleth not the things that be of the spirit of God, for it is foolishness to him.

We all have some kinship to St. Thomas's carnal-minded man in that the promise of a heavenly banquet means more to us than the promise that we shall shine as the sun, but both are metaphors, and in the last resort we must be content to accept what God has prepared for us. He knows what best befits our nature, seeing that He created it. St. John tells us that "they will not be hungry or thirsty any more" (Rev. 7:16), ruling out a literal banquet, and our Lord Himself had told us: "When the dead rise again, there is no marrying and giving in marriage; they are as the angels of God" (Matt. 22:30).

Though they are as the angels of God, they are yet men with body as well as soul, and the welcome God has prepared for those who love Him will be one that befits men. Does an angel, for instance, know the infinite gradation of shades that make up color? Can he appreciate what we mean by beauty of form, of harmony, of texture, of fragrance? The answer would seem to be that an angel knows these things in their causes, but he cannot perceive them precisely as we perceive them with our senses. Now, if purely sensual pleasures are excluded from the promise, it is not so much that we are deprived of anything we could desire as that we shall no longer desire such pleasures when we realize at last and possess our true good. But the very fact of the resurrection of the body seems to imply that the higher pleasures of the senses, which even on earth can raise our minds to God, will not be wanting in the new heaven and the new earth. We may recall that on the one authentic occasion when poor mortals were granted a glimpse of a corner of heaven, it was to see the heavenly choir and to hear the *Gloria in excelsis Deo*, though the Gospel does say that the angels were saying, not singing, the Gloria. St. John, in his visions in Revelation, heard canticles and saw the harps that have laid the foundation for the tradition of heavenly music. It is a thing that makes little appeal to some of us, but perhaps all that will be changed when our voices, and our ears too, are perfected.

However, it is idle for us to speculate on what lies so much beyond our experience and our intelligence. What we shall look for in that transformed and elevated life, we do not know, but we can be quite sure of this, that we shall not be disappointed. God has promised us that we shall enter heaven body and soul; God knows, and we do not know, the welcome most adapted to our nature that He has prepared for us.

NINE

The Incidental Joys of Heaven

THIS chapter deals with the incidental joys of heaven. We give them this name to distinguish them from the Beatific Vision, which is the essential joy of heaven and with which they are not worthy to be compared. It may seem illogical to dwell, after considering the Beatific Vision, on any other joy. Illogical perhaps it is, yet there is this to be said for it, that precisely because these joys are so much lower, they are therefore so much more within our ken, so much more within reach of our imagination. Besides, they are put before us in Holy Scripture where we are told that the happiness of the blessed will be complete and unalloyed and free from any of those shadows that never cease to threaten us on earth.

Whimsically interpreting St. Thomas Aquinas, Maurice Baring tells us:[2]

---

[2] Maurice Baring, *Round the World in Any Number of Days.* It is only fair to the memory of Maurice Baring to mention that, in this passage, he is concerned primarily not to describe the Beatific Vision but to convey to ignorant readers the taste of a ripe mango.

The point of the Beatific Vision, writes St. Thomas, is its *infinite variety.* So that those who enjoy it have at the same time the feeling that they are looking at a perfect landscape, hearing the sweetest music, bathing in a cool stream on a hot day, reaching the top of a mountain, galloping on grass on a horse that isn't running away, floating over tree-tops in a balloon, reading good verse, eating toasted cheese, drinking a really good cocktail—and any other nice thing you can think of, *all at once.*

Having studied his St. Thomas, Maurice Baring would know that the Angelic Doctor teaches quite firmly that the more sensual delights will be ours, not literally and in themselves but preeminently and in a more excellent way. He rightly emphasizes, with St. Thomas, the two points of the infinite variety of the joys of heaven and the simultaneous enjoyment of them all. For in the Beatific Vision, we possess the source of every good and in it therefore we can find satisfaction for every faculty and exercise for every aptitude of our nature. If sensual pleasures are wanting, it is only because, as St. Augustine says, they are the pleasures of sickness and not of health; in heaven, we shall recognize that they are not true goods, and we shall be without any desire for them. Further, we shall have all the joys of heaven simultaneously, all at once. In our limited earthly life, we can cope with only one thing at a time: these joys will come to a nature expanded to receive them, bringing to it perfect bliss.

What, then, are these added joys of heaven? In chapter 7 we have already dealt with the joy that the intellect can find in a study of Providence and its ways, in an understanding of all human history, of nature and its laws, of the universe created by God and its evolution: all natural knowledge will be an open book before us. In chapter 8, we mentioned the delights of the senses and speculated on how far they are appropriate to heaven, coming to the tentative conclusion that while sensual pleasure is to be excluded, the higher pleasures of the senses are not. We might perhaps put it in this way, that mere animal sensual pleasure can find no place in heaven but a sensual pleasure that is also truly intellectual—beauty in all its forms—will be ours, to delight the senses of the risen body.

I

St. John in Revelation enumerates some of our joys: "They will not be hungry or thirsty any more; no sun, no noonday heat, shall fall across their path. The Lamb, who dwells where the throne is, will be their shepherd, leading them out to the springs whose water is life; and God will wipe away every tear from their eyes" (Rev. 7:16-17). "Blessed are the dead who die in the Lord. Yes, for ever henceforward, the Spirit says; they are to have rest from their labours; but the deeds they did in life go with them now" (Rev. 14:13). "Here is God's tabernacle pitched among men; he will dwell with them, and they will be his own people, and he will be among them, their own God. He will wipe away every tear from their eyes, and there will be no more death, or mourning, or cries of distress, no more sorrow; those old things have passed away" (Rev. 21:3-4). We shall dwell on each of the promises made here, though we are conscious that in the more positive statements, St. John maintains the vagueness and symbolism that make it impossible for us to form a picture of heaven. However, even in the negative promises of the absence of evils, there is held out to us the hope of positive well-being in an unencumbered life.

But first there is salvation itself, the joy of being saved. The very word reminds us that while we are in this life, we are in danger of falling through our own weakness, we are in peril of hell. That peril frightens us at times, but not nearly as much as it should, and it is only when we are at last saved that we shall realize the imminence and the terror of the peril. We have had experience of such things as the moment of panic when we are crossing a street and suddenly find a car upon us, the panic and the immediate relief of escape; or of a bombing and the deliverance of the all clear; or of a war that threatened our very life issuing in victory. What then must be the final sense of relief when this life, with the tremendous weight of eternity upon it, shakes off its burden and wins its crown! Men have fainted with relief at a danger passed: shall we spend eternity gasping? The answer is that this will be no mere escape from a terrible fate; rather, it will be the accomplishment of a task beyond our powers, a success for which we scarcely dared to hope, victory in the fight that was set before us. It will not be so much hell escaped as heaven gained, and a heaven beyond our dreams.

"They will not be hungry or thirsty any more; no sun, no noonday heat, will fall across their path." The first of these promises we have already dealt with; the second will not immediately appeal to those who welcome the infrequent warmth of a northern sky and have no experience of the hostile glare of a tropical sun. But taking them together, we may see in them the hope of an end to the discomforts of life that means the real beginning of human life as it should be, as it would have been if Adam had not sinned. Our life now is dominated by Original Sin and its effects: our wills are weak, our minds are clouded, our powers infirm; our efforts fail constantly to reach the goal we aim at. If we rely on others, they disappoint us; the very elements conspire against us. Nothing is quite right, everything is awry: we are too hot or too cold, too early or too late, too weak or too strong; we are always putting up with a second best. Adam, before his fall, dominating creation—that is the proper human life: that is to be ours, but more perfectly even than it was for Adam.

"For ever henceforward they are to rest from their labours." Only in heaven shall we know how we have had to labor, what that curse of Adam has meant to each one of us: "Thou hast listened to thy wife's counsel and hast eaten the fruit I forbade thee to eat; and now, through thy act, the ground is under a curse. All the days of thy life thou shalt win food from it with toil; thorns and thistles it shall yield thee, this ground from which thou dost win thy food. Still shalt thou earn thy bread with the sweat of thy brow" (Gen. 3:17–19). What labors we have known and how weary they have made us! Even if we have not tilled the ground, the struggle for a livelihood occupies most of our lives, and whatever the means we take to it, there is the same frustration and round of disappointments. For most people, the daily work by which they earn their living is a burden that fills their lives, and with the hours they must give to taking their meals and to sleep, they are left with little time for anything else. And so much of our effort proves useless, our efforts to do good even, our efforts to improve ourselves, our struggles with evil. How weary they make us! As one gets older, one gets very tired, and when death comes at last, after a long sickness, it seems to be not unwelcome, because it is met with utter weariness. Oh, to have rest from our labors!

Against this, Sir Arnold Lunn has said that he cannot conceive of a heaven without the sensation of effort crowned, such as the mountaineer enjoys in struggling to a summit. To this, one can answer that in salvation, as we have seen, there is the triumph of scaling the cliff of heaven—and the joys of heaven are not transitory, but eternal. Yet Sir Arnold is surely right in arguing that heaven is not to be regarded as a place of rest. Without activity, there is no life, and therefore the repose of heaven is not like the collapse of exhaustion, nor the reaction after great effort, but the vigor of a life that will know no weariness. Again, while it is true that in this life we do experience great pleasure in striving toward a goal, and exaltation when we attain it, we cannot safely argue from that, because in this life we do not know perfection, the absolute Good; we are content with small mercies. In heaven it will be far otherwise. Since pleasure comes from a faculty perfectly exercised in its proper function, then indeed pleasure will be ours, when every faculty, every aptitude of our nature, is perfected and exercised, fully alive in blissful activity.

"He will wipe away every tear from their eyes, and there will be no more death." This is a vale of tears, and we cannot conceive of a life without them. Tears are never very deep while we remain on earth, and it is stoicism or self-control, not happiness, that keeps them in check. Why, tears come even with joy, even with relief: Why is this? Is it that we know that the joy and the relief are momentary things? That which we feared, which has for the moment been deflected, must surely come and sorrow will catch up with us at last. There will be no more death. What sorrow death has brought and daily brings into our lives! We could not live with death, whether the thought of our own or the sight of that of others, were it not that our imaginations are so quickly dulled by time that we can find some sort of refuge in forgetfulness. Death it is that makes all happiness here a passing phase; only in the absence of death could heaven be heaven. God sees, and we in a vague way can also see, that heaven must be eternal. If we were promised a hundred years of bliss, or a thousand or ten thousand, it would not do; heaven would not be heaven if there was an inevitable curtain at the further end to blight our joy.

II

"There will be no more death, or mourning, or cries of distress, no more sorrow." Tears are shed perhaps more often and more bitterly over a bereavement than over anything else, and from the beginning Christians have found their consolation in the thought of heaven. "Make no mistake, brethren," writes St. Paul, "about those who have gone to their rest; you are not to lament over them, as the rest of the world does, with no hope to live by. We believe, after all, that Jesus underwent death and rose again; just so, when Jesus comes back, God will bring back those who have found rest through him" (1 Thess. 4:12–13). With that hope every Christian has consoled others and has been consoled himself ever since. "We shall all meet merrily in heaven," St. Thomas More told his daughter, Margaret. That we should mourn now is natural, but that we should look forward to being united in heaven is a special gift of our Lord to us. Here certainly, St. John's promise is not a negative one, but a positive joy and one we can appreciate. What a reunion it will be! In this life, there is always the fear of bereavement, of separation, the greater fear of disappointment, of finding the one loved unworthy, the fear of not being loved in return, of being oneself unworthy. For one who really loves our Lord, the greatest of afflictions is to see some dear friend or relative fall into sin and risk his eternal salvation, and the fervent prayers that such an occurrence inspires are often patently answered, as were the prayers of a Monica for an Augustine. In heaven these fears will have disappeared; there will be no fear of disappointment, for we shall see the perfection of those we love; no fear for ourselves, since we too shall be perfected and made completely worthy of love. The love we feel for family and friends, then, gives us a true foretaste of heaven. If, at times, our love tends to be selfish and unworthy of our Lord, He can and does purify it by affliction and bereavement. Is not the Christian family, which most of us have known, His way of bringing us to Himself, His way of saving us? Has He not laid on us His commandment that we should have love one for another, that we should love one another as He has loved us? Can we have any doubt, then, but that this life of love is destined to find its fulfillment and crown in heaven? The family will be one again; its merits, its joys, its secrets will be blessed by God. We shall all meet merrily in heaven.

If anyone seeks confirmation of this, he need only read St. John's account of our Lord's last night with His apostles before He suffered, for He too felt the love we feel for family and friends. "Before the paschal feast began, Jesus already knew that the time had come for his passage from this world to the Father. He still loved those who were his own, whom he was leaving in the world, and he would give them the uttermost proof of his love" (John 13:1). "I am going away to prepare a home for you. And though I do go away, to prepare you a home, I am coming back; and then I will take you to myself, so that you too may be where I am" (John 14:2–3). "I will not leave you friendless; I am coming to you" (John 14:18). "I do not speak of you any more as my servants; a servant is one who does not understand what his master is about, whereas I have made known to you all that my Father has told me; and so I have called you my friends" (John 15:15). "You are distressed now; but one day I will see you again, and then your hearts will be glad; and your gladness will be one which nobody can take away from you" (John 16:22), and finally, in His prayer to His Father: "This, Father, is my desire, that all those whom thou hast entrusted to me may be with me where I am.... I have revealed, and will reveal, thy name to them; so that the love thou hast bestowed upon me may dwell in them, and I, too, may dwell in them" (John 17:24,

26). This love of the Sacred Heart, embracing each of us, desiring to share His glory with us, is that revelation of heaven of which we spoke in chapter 6. Our human love, then, if we spiritualize it, loving those dear to us in Him and Him in them, is something not merely blessed by our Lord, but something already divine, which we shall take with us from this life to the eternal life to come.

"The deeds they did in life go with them now." This promise of the book of Revelation at least is not negative. St. John indicates that the martyrs and the virgins are singled out for special honor in heaven, but no doubt it is true that there is no service that has been rendered to our Divine Lord but will receive a great reward, and for each of the blessed there will be a special crown. He has told us that even a cup of cold water given in His name shall not be without its reward, and the reward comes not simply as some external prize but as a perfecting of the very soul, for a change in our surroundings would be little if we ourselves were not also changed. Even here on earth we have the desire for our own perfection and the yearning for personal distinction that tends to fill our daydreams with vain imaginings. They must be vain if we look in the wrong direction for perfection, or if we seek to attain it by our own efforts. But rightly viewed, this is the task that God has set us for our time of trial: the true perfecting of the nature He has given us by its rebirth and growth in Christ, by its increasing supernatural life. "You are to be perfect, as your heavenly Father is perfect" (Matt. 5:48) was the seemingly impossible standard our Lord set before us; in heaven we shall know what His words mean, enjoying through eternity that share in the divine nature that, by His grace, He accomplished in us on earth. Every cup of cold water given in His name, every supernatural act we do, of thought or word or deed — and every action of our lives that is not sinful can be supernatural — builds up our life in Christ. We said earlier that every chance of merit lost is lost forever, and now we can see what that loss is: it is a grace lost, some growth in Christ lost, some eternal perfection of our being lost. Entering heaven, the deeds we did on earth go with us now; it is our past lives that make us what we are, and as we differ in the details of our past supernatural life, so we are distinguished now. Each of us will be individual, unique, like no other soul, adorned with our own accumulation of supernatural grace. In heaven this supernatural grace will give place to the new garment of the soul, the *lumen gloriae*, which enables us to look on God. This again will be unique, our own, merited by each of us through Christ. Our faculties now will be tuned to perfect activity, perfectly apt for their function, continuously and perfectly exercised; our minds free from error, free from deception, clear, certain, powerful, grasping truth and having Truth itself within their grasp; our wills, no longer wayward, but indomitable, fixed in good and having Good itself within their reach; body and soul, at last in harmony, with powers developed to the full and exercised integrally; our whole nature caught up and divinized, yet not changed into something else. We shall still be ourselves, yet such as we never conceived, realizing now at last the nobility of man. The Lamb will be our shepherd leading us out to the springs whose water is life. We have followed Him from afar: now we are His companions and His friends, and He is making it, as He promised, His care to give us welcome and to provide for us all that our nature could desire.

It is thus transformed that we shall go to meet the saints of God, our family and friends, but a multitude of new friends too: we have not exhausted the possibilities of friendship on earth. There are first the friends we have known afar off, our patrons to whom we have prayed for help. We cannot but think of them as far off still, far above us, but "you are no longer exiles, then, or aliens;

the saints are your fellow citizens, you belong to God's household" (Eph. 2:19). We know the joy of companionship. When we think of the saints, their number and their nobility, we must feel that, if there were no other joy in heaven, this would be bliss to spend eternity in such company and fellowship. We have to remind our-selves that this is only one of the lesser, incidental joys deriving from the fact that God will dwell with them and they will be his people and he will be among them, their own God.

To the saints are added the hosts of God's angels; they too will be our fellow citizens and friends. More than once in Scripture, we read of an angel sent as a messenger to man, and of the man, dazzled by such beauty, falling down to adore him, thinking that this must be God Himself (cf. e.g., Rev. 22:8). Pure spirits, they show forth the power and wisdom of God in their various perfec-tions and powers. With them, too, we could find occupation and pleasure through eternity. Our guardian angel will no doubt be waiting for us, and there will be immediate occasion for mutual congratulations that the time of trial is at last successfully passed. Are there jokes in heaven? I cannot see how there can be in that clear light, for in a joke there is always something of an error; yet perhaps when our guardian angel tells us of the scrapes we missed through him, of his steering us just clear of pitfalls, we shall laugh together at the fool he had to deal with. I do not know.

Then there is the Queen of Heaven—what is one to say of her? She certainly will not be far above us, Queen though she is of God's creatures. We can talk to her as to our own faithful mother, by whom we have been saved. We shall want to hear from her own lips the story of our redemption, of the Annunciation, the Visitation to Elizabeth a few days later, when the Child in her womb sanctified His precursor, of Bethlehem and His birth, of Egypt and then the long, happy years at Nazareth; we have much to learn of these; of Calvary, too, that crowning glory among the works of God; of her life afterwards, and of her life through the ages, Mother of the brethren of Christ; of her motherhood of us. Looking back upon our lives on earth, we shall find, I hope, that the words we spoke most often were these: Hail Mary, full of grace, the Lord is with thee; blessed art thou among women and blessed is the fruit of thy womb, Jesus. Holy Mary, Mother of God, pray for us sinners now and at the hour of our death. She will know each of the Hail Mary's and can tell us her answer to each. Will it be for Mary to lead us to her Son? I think it must be, and then at last we shall hear that voice: "Well done, thou good and faithful servant," and He will make us free of His kingdom, and we can say with the Psalmist: "No, it is the Lord I claim for my prize, the Lord who fills my cup; thou and no other will ensure my inheritance to me. No fairer lot could be mine; no nobler inheritance could I win" (Ps. 15:5–6).

TEN

The Achievement

⟨━━━━━━ ······ ━━━━━━⟩

W E have called this chapter "The Achievement" because in it we look forward to the end of the world, to the completion of the human story, the consummation of our redemption. It is the story of the personal achievement of our Blessed Lord, and the chapter therefore is concerned primarily with His work, what He has accomplished in us.

It is curious to note that we seem, now that the world is getting old, to look for its end with less expectancy than did our fathers. Some of the early Christians, as we learn from St. Paul (2 Thess. 2:2) were terrified of the approaching end; St. Leo thought he read the signs of it in the crumbling Roman Empire, and a hundred and fifty years later Gregory the Great noted many portents of approaching doom. So, through the ages, others have seen signs of the end of the world. In recent centuries, it has not been so. Perhaps it was the expansion of the horizons of the known world, making it clear that much more remained to be done in the propagation of the gospel; perhaps it was that faith had grown cold; but, whatever the reason, the end of the world has seemed to recede. Yet if St. Gregory lived in our modern age, we cannot doubt that he would be even more insistent in his warnings. However this may be, our Lord would have us think of the end, and He has put before us a picture of it that is firm in its details, when compared, for instance, with the detail we have of heaven itself. The day is coming, and He warns us it will come when we do not expect it. "But as for that day and that hour you speak of, they are known to none, not even to the angels of heaven; only the Father knows them" (Matt. 24:36).

One is tempted to speculate on how the coming of that day must appear to the souls in heaven, but this is something we cannot imagine, and it is idle to try to do so. It seems clear that the disembodied souls, perfectly happy though they are, must look for their own completion and the resurrection of their bodies, but how the interval between their death and glorification and the day passes, we do not know at all. Time, as we know it, cannot exist for them: there will be no fast movement, nor slow, no waiting impatiently. There is first this state of disembodied souls, and then in due time there follows the other.

We are not, however, in this chapter, concerned with the signs of the approaching end, nor even with the judgment that follows them. Our object is to consider the personal triumph of our Redeemer. For one thing is central about all what we are told of that day: it is the day of the Lord. The Son of Man will come again, a second time; He will come in majesty and power, like the lightning that springs up from the east and flashes across to the west; all his angels will be about Him, the trumpet of God sounding; He will sit on the throne of His glory and judge the world; He will be acknowledged by all and will lead the blessed into the kingdom prepared for them. It is remarkable how frequently we find mention of the second coming and triumph of our Lord in St. Paul, St. Peter, St. Jude, St. John. A book on heaven would be incomplete if we did not dwell on it.

There is one passage in particular in St. Paul where he deals at some length with the significance of this day; it is in that fifteenth chapter of the first Epistle to the Corinthians, much of which we have already quoted. There he writes:

Just as all have died with Adam, so with Christ all will be brought to life. But each must rise in his own rank; Christ is the first-fruits, and after him follow those who belong to him, those who have put their trust in his return. Full completion comes after that, when he places his kingship in the hands of God, his Father, having first dispossessed every other sort of rule, authority, and power; his reign, as we know, must continue until he has put all his enemies under his feet, and the last of those enemies to be dispossessed is death. God has put all things in subjection under his feet; that is, all things have been made subject to him, except indeed that power which made them his subjects. And when that subjection is complete, then the Son himself will become subject to the power which made all things his subjects, so that God may be all in all. (1 Cor. 15:22–28)

These words clearly carry us into the high mystery of the Incarnation and Redemption. They seem to teach that Christ's kingdom is a temporary one, but, on the other hand, the angel had said to Mary at the Annunciation: "His kingdom shall never have an end" (Luke 1:33). The meaning therefore rather is that this kingdom is in process of being established until the day of the Lord. The Father sent His Son into a rebellious world, that He might conquer evil and win for Himself a kingdom. When finally this is accomplished, He will lay His authority and His kingdom at the feet of His Father, and God will be all in all. We will try then to see what this task is that was given to our Lord, God made man, and what it is that He has achieved. In a sense, this whole book has been about that, but here we will gather the threads together and summarize the story.

I

Our Lord Himself made use of that word, *achieved*, completed, consummated, in His prayer to the Father, after the Supper, but before the Agony, when He had offered Himself to death for us: "Father, the time has come; give glory now to thy Son, that thy Son may give glory to thee. Thou hast put him in authority over all mankind, to bring eternal life to all those thou hast entrusted to him. Eternal life is knowing thee, who art the only true God, and Jesus Christ, whom thou hast sent. I have exalted thy glory on earth, by achieving the task which thou gavest me to do" (John 17:1-4). He has, He says, achieved the task His Father gave Him to do, bringing eternal life to all those entrusted to Him. He had completed His task when as our High Priest He offered Himself to death for us; it remained for others to lead Him like a lamb to the slaughter in the Passion, which was just about to begin. Next day, when the Passion, too, was complete, just before He bowed His head in death, He made use of that word again, saying: "It is achieved." His task was done. What, then, was this task? Holy Scripture repeatedly makes this clear: there was a double element in it, first to make satisfaction for our sins, and so to open heaven to us, secondly to bring us to heaven by communicating to us His own Sonship. "It was God's good pleasure to let all completeness dwell in him, and through him to win back all things, whether on earth or in heaven, into union with himself, making peace with them through his blood, shed on the cross" (Col. 1:19-20). Here we have the double aspect of the Redemption: God would make peace with men, and He would win them back into union with Himself.

When Adam sinned, he lost supernatural life, which God had given him, lost it for himself and for his children, for he had been constituted head of the human race. Men continued to pile sin on sin, and the whole race was at enmity with God. God had made man for His own great glory; man refused to give Him glory. He had made man free, demanding from him free service; man refused to serve. God might have condoned these offenses, but in fact He demanded the fullest reparation, and since man was utterly incapable of making reparation himself, God sent His only-begotten Son into the world to heal the enmity between God and man.

We must pause here to notice that when, following Scripture, we talk of enmity, we are speaking of the cause of enmity that our sins are, for God's enmity was of such a kind as to move Him to give us His greatest favor by sending to us His only-begotten Son. Should we wonder, then, when our Lord tells us to love our enemies?

Our Lord came then, first, to make satisfaction for our sins. The angel, announcing His coming, told Mary to call His name Jesus, Savior; and again, to St. Joseph: "She will bear a son, whom thou shalt call Jesus, for he is to save his people from their sins" (Matt. 1:21). The Word of God was made flesh and dwelt amongst us, fully a man, like to us in all things, sin alone excepted. Like Adam, He was constituted by God head of the human race that He might repair the fault of Adam: "Thou hast put him in authority over all mankind" (John 17:2). He was the High Priest, the Mediator, appointed to approach God on behalf of men to offer reparation for our sins. His offering was the sacrifice of His own body and blood, for He was the victim, too, in the sacrifice: "This is my blood, of the new testament, shed for many, to the remission of sins" (Matt. 26:28); "What was the ransom that freed you?... It was paid in the precious blood of Christ" (1 Pet. 1:18–19).

In His sacrifice, there was not only the offering of His life's blood. Our sins were sins because of our rebellion against the will of God: we would not serve: we would not render glory to our Creator. The only-begotten Son of God, made man, served on behalf of mankind: He was made obedient unto death, even to the death of the Cross. His offering was a sign, a proof, of His complete submission to the Father's will. In Him and through Him, mankind offered glory, gave service, to the Creator. God and man were at peace.

Thus it was that He not only made satisfaction for our sins but also merited for us the grace by which we might be saved; not only opened heaven to us but also gave to us the life and the strength to travel the road to heaven. He merited for us, or more truly, He merited for Himself the right to communicate His life to us that we, too, might be sons of God. "Our sins had made dead men of us, and he, in giving life to Christ, gave life to us too; it is his grace that has saved you; raised us up too, enthroned us too above the heavens, in Christ Jesus" (Eph. 2:5–6) and again: "Christ died for us all, so that being alive should no longer mean living with our own life, but with his life who died for us and has risen again" (2 Cor. 5:15). This means clearly that Christ's task was not completed with His death: in the plan of the Redemption we were not to be passive beneficiaries of His sacrifice. Lifted up on the Cross, He would draw all things to Himself, sharing with us His life, so that in us and through us, He could continue to overcome sin and evil, continue to serve the Father, and continue to merit heaven. To see the full scope of His achievement, we must follow the life of our Lord, in His glory.

II

After our Lord died on the Cross, we are told in the Creed that He descended into hell, that is, not the hell of the damned but that limbo where the souls of the just had gone, from the time of Adam onwards, until heaven should be opened to men. To them, then, He showed Himself, and they learnt to know their Redeemer, learnt the source of the grace by which they had served God in life, saw the Man who had paid their ransom and merited for them life, the Man who had been their life. He had, though they had not fully known it, even before He took human nature, by God's anticipation of the plentiful Redemption, been their Savior. In a little while the penitent thief came to join Him in paradise, for paradise had now begun for these souls, though they must await the resurrection of their bodies until the day of the Lord.

For when we say that mankind was at enmity with God through sin, we must remember that no sooner was the first sin committed, and mankind left without hope, than God took the means to repair the evil. He promised to Adam a Redeemer, and the grace that Christ merited on the Cross was given to Adam, to Eve, and to all their descendants. Thus the way of salvation was opened to them. Heaven indeed was closed: no man could enter it, and those who, through the grace of Christ, were saved, must wait until He, the first of many brethren, should enter.

For us others who came after, there is not only the inestimable grace of knowing Him and knowing His life, but also there is, what is much more, a share in His life, a share in His work of Redemption. Our Lord, in paying the price of our redemption, had not swept away the evil in the world. The effects of Original Sin were to remain, but it was no longer too much for man, since over against it was the strength of Christ. He saw, no doubt, that the evil we could now, through His grace, fight and conquer, would be a source of our greater merit and future glory. We were to show ourselves the sons of God by the weapons we should use. To fight with the world's weapons would be nothing; to fight with the weapons of Christ, weakness, suffering, humiliation, death itself, to fight and to win; only the children of God could do that. He left us His sacraments through which His life might be nourished. He left us the Sacrifice of the Mass, through which we might offer up to God the spotless Victim, rendering to Him a gift worthy of God Himself. He left us suffering and the cross that we might show the powerlessness of evil against the weakness of the cross.

Christ, our Lord, risen in glory and ascended to the Father, was to reign gloriously in heaven, but it was His will to live on also on earth in His members, and in them continue to achieve his task. This metaphor of the head and the members, which St. Paul frequently develops, is an exact parallel of our Lord's own metaphor of the vine and the branches. We have spoken of them before, considering what they meant to us, but now we shall look at them rather, as it were, from the side of Christ, so that we may grasp more fully His achievement. In the Letter to the Romans, St. Paul says: "Each of us has one body, with many different parts, and not all these parts have the same function; just so we, though many in number, form one body in Christ" (Rom. 12:4–5). Here we have the essential element of the metaphor: we are the members, or limbs, or organs, the parts of the Body of Christ. The idea behind the metaphor is explained at some length in the twelfth chapter of the First Letter to the Corinthians; its application to our Lord is best pressed home in the Letter to the Ephesians:

> You are one body with a single Spirit; each of you, when he was called, called in the same hope; with the same

Lord, the same faith, the same baptism; with the same God, the same Father, all of us, who is above all beings, pervades all things, and lives in all of us.... Some he has appointed to be apostles, others to be prophets, others to be evangelists, or pastors, or teachers. They are to order the lives of the faithful, minister to their needs, build up the frame of Christ's body, until we all realize our common unity through faith in the Son of God, and fuller knowledge of him. So we shall reach perfect manhood, that maturity which is proportioned to the completed growth of Christ.... We are to follow the truth in a spirit of charity, and so grow up, in everything, into a due proportion with Christ, who is our head. On him all the body depends; it is organized and unified by each contact with the source which supplies it; and thus each limb receiving the active power it needs, it achieves its natural growth, building itself up through charity. (Eph. 4:4–16)

This then was to be the scope of His achievement. He was to continue to live on earth, giving life to His members. All who heard His call were to enter into His Body, of which the Spirit of God was the soul. Each organ—that is, each individual Christian—must itself develop and grow to perfect maturity, drawing its life from Christ, who is the head. The different organs, each performing its proper function in the whole body, each growing to its individual perfection, together contribute to the development of the whole body to perfect manhood. The organs, the members, whether considered separately or together, derive their life and their growth from Christ. The Body then is Christ's Body; it is Christ who is growing; the life is Christ's life. As Christ lived in the world and overcame evil, His Body must overcome the evil of the world. As

Christ suffered and so entered into His glory, His members and each member must suffer and so attain heaven. As Christ merited for His Church, His members, too, must "pay off the debt which the afflictions of Christ still leave to be paid for the sake of his body, the Church." When this Body of Christ was grown to full manhood, to perfect stature, then the day of the Lord would come, but that day and that hour only God knows.

As we said earlier, to speak of this as the Mystical Body of Christ does not at all imply that it is an unreal body. The Mystical Body is not a material body, but it is so real that we can say positively that it is only through membership of that Body, only because we are grafted on to Christ, that we can hope to enter heaven. So with the vine and the branches, we can assert that neither in this life nor in the next can we live if we are separated from the vinestock. These are metaphors, but they are metaphors divinely chosen to express a truth that human words strive in vain to convey.

It is impossible for us to exaggerate what we owe to Jesus Christ, our Lord. He is our Savior, for "this alone of all the names under heaven has been appointed to men as the one by which we must needs be saved" (Acts 4:12). He is the way to heaven: "Nobody can come to the Father, except through me" (John 14:6). He is the Truth: "What I was born for, what I came into the world for, is to bear witness of the truth. Whoever belongs to the truth, listens to my voice" (John 18:37). He is Life: "I have come that they may have life and have it more abundantly" (John 10:10), and: "If a man lives on in me and I in him, then he will yield abundant fruit; separated from me, you have no power to do anything" (John 15:5). It is not we who live, but Christ who lives in us.

We are not exaggerating this union of our souls with Christ, for how else could we explain what we have been asserting in this book. The enormity of the claim that these bodies of ours will die, fall into decay, and then rise glorious and immortal, this is a mere nothing to our other claims. We asserted that we merit heaven, that we have a right in justice to heaven, that God must give it to us as a fitting crown for our work. And what is this heaven that we claim so confidently? It is nothing less than union with God Himself. We shall see Him face-to-face, penetrating that impenetrable light. We shall be taken up into the life of love that is the life of the Blessed Trinity.

We are not exaggerating the achievement of Christ, for how could we when we consider the means by which He brought it about. God sent His only-begotten Son into the world as a man. God's wisdom found that a necessary means for what He would accomplish. The Son of God lived as a man and died for us. Christ's continuing life in us is nourished by His physical Body and Blood, coming down on our altars from heaven, to be received into our bodies, that we may be assimilated to Him. These are some of the means required to achieve what? To achieve what we have here set down, briefly, inadequately. The truth is something greater than words can express.

When Christ has grown to perfect manhood, then He will come again in glory. "His reign, as we know," says St. Paul, "must continue until he has put all his enemies under his feet, and the last of these enemies to be dispossessed is death." When in the last of His members, He has won the long struggle with sin and evil, that will be the day of the Lord. Then death, too, will be conquered and "he will form this humbled body of ours anew, moulding it into the image of his glorified body, so effective is his power to make all things obey him" (Phil. 3:21). Body and soul, complete men again, those whom He washed clean in His blood, those whose life He has been, go to meet their Redeemer, their head, "a great multitude past all counting, taken from all nations and tribes and peoples and languages" (Rev. 7:9). In Christ and with Christ and through Christ, this multitude has served and glorified God. In spite of sin and evil they have triumphed; they have overcome the world, overcome the devil, walking as children of God should walk. This is the kingdom of God among men; this is the Body of Christ.

These He leads into the house of His Father, who for this had sent Him into the world. Bringing this company, His Body, His Bride, before the throne of God, He will say finally: "Father, I have achieved the task thou gavest me to do," and God will be all in all.

Sophia Institute

Sophia Institute is a nonprofit institution that seeks to nurture the spiritual, moral, and cultural life of souls and to spread the Gospel of Christ in conformity with the authentic teachings of the Roman Catholic Church.

Sophia Institute Press fulfills this mission by offering translations, reprints, and new publications that afford readers a rich source of the enduring wisdom of mankind.

Sophia Institute also operates the popular online Catholic resource CatholicExchange.com. *Catholic Exchange* provides world news from a Catholic perspective as well as daily devotionals and articles that will help readers to grow in holiness and live a life consistent with the teachings of the Church.

In 2013, Sophia Institute launched Sophia Institute for Teachers to renew and rebuild Catholic culture through service to Catholic education. With the goal of nurturing the spiritual, moral, and cultural life of souls, and an abiding respect for the role and work of teachers, we strive to provide materials and programs that are at once enlightening to the mind and ennobling to the heart; faithful and complete, as well as useful and practical.

Sophia Institute gratefully recognizes the Solidarity Association for preserving and encouraging the growth of our apostolate over the course of many years. Without their generous and timely support, this book would not be in your hands.

www.SophiaInstitute.com
www.CatholicExchange.com
www.SophiaInstituteforTeachers.org

Sophia Institute Press® is a registered trademark of Sophia Institute.
Sophia Institute is a tax-exempt institution as defined by the
Internal Revenue Code, Section 501(c)(3). Tax I.D. 22-2548708.